pred	faulty predication **40**
quot	quotation marks placed improperly in relation to punctuation mark **80, 81, 82**
ref	faulty pronoun reference **24**
rep	careless repetition **47**
restr	punctuate a restrictive clause properly **65**
sp	spelling error
title	improper format of title for published work **83, 84**
trite	trite expression **44**
vb	improper form of verb **33**
wdy	wordy sentence **46**
ww	wrong word **40**

PROOFREADERS' MARKS

⌒	close up space		
⌐	delete		
⌐	delete and close up space		
#	separate with a space		
∧	insert here what is indicated in the margin		
¶	start new paragraph		
no ¶	no paragraph; run in with previous paragraph		
⊙ /	insert period	*cap*	use capital letter here
⋀ /	insert comma	*lc*	use lowercase letter here
; /	insert semicolon	*ital*	set in italic type
: /	insert colon	*rom*	set in roman type
$\frac{1}{M}$ /	insert em dash	*sc*	set in small capitals
$\frac{1}{M}$ / $\frac{1}{M}$	insert pair of em dashes	*bf*	set in boldface type
= /	insert hyphen	*tr*	transpose letters
' /	insert apostrophe		or words

Fifth Edition

THE LITTLE ENGLISH HANDBOOK
CHOICES AND CONVENTIONS

Edward P. J. Corbett

THE OHIO STATE UNIVERSITY

SCOTT, FORESMAN AND COMPANY

Glenview, Illinois   London, England

This book is dedicated to all my students over the years, whose written prose sometimes mystified me, often enlightened me, and invariably beguiled me. Bless them all.

Acknowledgments

Adapted excerpts from *Structural Essentials of English* by Harold Whitehall, copyright, 1954, © 1956 by Harcourt Brace Jovanovich, Inc. Reprinted by permission of the publisher.

Library of Congress Cataloging-in-Publication Data

Corbett, Edward P. J.
  The Little English Handbook.
  Includes index.
    1. English language—Rhetoric—Handbooks, manuals, etc.   2. English language—Usage—Handbooks, manuals, etc.   I. Title.
PE1408.C587   1987   808'.042   86–21987
ISBN 0–673–18474–9

PREFACE TO THE FIFTH EDITION

The Little English Handbook is designed to serve as a guide on basic matters of grammar, style, paragraphing, punctuation, and mechanics for those engaged in writing public prose. By "public prose," I mean that dialect of written English most commonly used in the newspapers, magazines, and books that the majority of educated native speakers read. This dialect ranges in style from the formal to the casual, from the literary to the colloquial. But because public prose has to be intelligible to a general audience, it avoids the esoteric vocabulary of various professional, regional, and social groups, and it observes the rules of grammar as taught in the schools.

The use of the term *public prose* is not intended to disparage the other current dialects, most of which serve well the needs of some of the people all of the time and all of the people some of the time. Obviously, spoken English, with its own wide range of professional, regional, and social dialects, serves the needs of more people more often than written English does. However, despite the primacy of the spoken language, there are occasions when many, if not most, native speakers must use the written language in order to record or communicate their thoughts, needs, and feelings. It is for those occasions that this handbook was prepared.

A HANDBOOK FOR COMMON PROBLEMS

Ever since the first edition of this handbook, I have concentrated on those matters of grammar, style, paragraphing, punctuation, and mechanics that from years of experience in reading student papers and responding to telephone queries from people in business and the professions, I know to be the most common and persistent problems in the expressive part of the writing process. For answers to the larger and more subtle problems in writing prose, you will have to consult one of the larger handbooks. I do not, for instance, provide guidance in all the uses of the comma; some of these uses are never or only seldom a problem for writers. Instead, I deal only with those half dozen conventions of the comma that are most often ignored or misused and that are most crucial for the preservation of clarity. If you master these six uses, you can rest assured that there are no really serious mistakes that you can make in the use (or the omission) of the comma.

CHOICES AND CONVENTIONS

The subtitle of this handbook, *Choices and Conventions*, reflects my approach to the matters I deal with. Some of the principles governing the system of writing have been established by convention; others represent a recommendation from a number of options. Accordingly, in most cases, I have stated the guiding principle in definite, unequivocal terms. I am the first to concede, however, that in matters of language, there should be no absolute prescriptions or proscriptions. Where choices are available, you must be guided in making your selection by a consideration of the subject matter, occasion, desired effect, and audience. But in my experience, those who need the guidance of a handbook want a simple, straightforward answer to their query.

PRIORITIES IN THE WRITING PROCESS

By concentrating on matters of grammar, style, paragraphing, punctuation, and mechanics, I do not wish to imply that these are the most important concerns of "good writing." What is most necessary for effective communication is the substance, originality, and sophistication of your thoughts and the ability to organize your thoughts in a unified, coherent way. Inept articulation of your thoughts, however, is often a reflection of inept processes of invention and organization. Careless expression stems ultimately from careless thinking. Observance of the "basics" treated in this handbook will not guarantee that your prose will be interesting to read or worth reading, but observance of the fundamental conventions of the writing system will at least guarantee that your prose can be read. Readable prose is no mean achievement. The next achievement to strive for is to write prose that others will want to read.

THE FIFTH EDITION

In previous editions of this handbook, I made a few additions and modifications in response to requests from users of the text. I have retained most of those changes in this edition, and I have made a few additional changes:

- The style has been fine-tuned throughout the text, mainly in the direction of making the prose easier for the user to read and understand.
- The section on Using the Library has been transferred from my *Little Rhetoric and Handbook* to the handbook in order to make the section on the research paper a more self-contained unit than it was in previous editions.
- The new MLA style of parenthetical documentation and the new MLA bibliographical style for the *Works Cited* page have been incorporated into this edition.
- The sample research paper exemplifies the new MLA style of documentation and bibliography.
- Some new samples of a résumé and a business letter have replaced the samples in previous editions.

I have heroically persisted in my resistance to the many

tempting suggestions I have received for substantial additions to the text because I wanted to keep the book relatively "little."

ACKNOWLEDGMENTS

Every textbook designed for classroom use profits from the criticisms and suggestions of experienced, knowledgeable teachers. The list of teachers who reviewed the manuscript of the first edition, of those who provided detailed critiques of subsequent editions, and of those who buttonholed me at conventions to offer me their suggestions for improving the text would be a long one indeed. My resorting to a collective word of appreciation here is not intended to minimize my feelings of gratitude to those teachers whose suggestions greatly improved previous editions. This fifth edition is likewise the product of my careful attention to the comments and suggestions of many teachers and students.

The author of any textbook also owes a great debt of gratitude to many people on the staff of his publisher—not only the people in the Editorial department but also the people in the Design, the Production, and the Promotion departments. If I were to acknowledge by name all those on the staff of Scott, Foresman to whom I am indebted, this list would extend for another two inches or more. But I would like to single out for special mention and a hearty thank-you Anne Smith, Constance Rajala, Hope Rajala, and Lydia Webster. They encouraged me and helped me at every stage of the project, but if there are any instances of ineptitude or wrongheadedness in the text, I am solely and culpably responsible for them.

Edward P. J. Corbett

CONTENTS

PUNCTUATION

MECHANICS

NEVER-SAY NEVERISMS

FORMAT OF THE RESEARCH PAPER

FORMS FOR LETTERS

LEGEND

Some of the conventions presented in this handbook, especially those having to do with punctuation, are illustrated with graphic models using these symbols:

A word inside the box designates a particular part of speech, e.g., | noun |.

 = word

A phrase is a meaningful combination of two or more words that does not constitute a clause.

_____ = phrase

The following abbreviations on the horizontal line designate a particular kind of phrase, e.g., ___prep.___.

   prep. = prepositional phrase (**on the bus**)
   part. = participial phrase (**having ridden on the bus**)
   ger. = gerund phrase (**riding on the bus** pleased him)
   inf. = infinitive phrase (he wanted **to ride on the bus**)

An independent clause, sometimes referred to as a main clause, can stand by itself as a grammatically complete sen-

tence, e.g., **He rode on the bus.** The vertical line indicates
the separation of subject from predicate.

‾‾‾‾‾‾‾‾‾‾‾┼‾‾‾‾‾‾‾‾‾‾‾ = independent (main) clause

A dependent clause, sometimes referred to as a subordinate clause, cannot stand by itself as a grammatically complete sentence.

┐‾‾‾‾‾‾‾‾‾‾‾┼‾‾‾‾‾‾‾‾‾‾‾ = dependent (subordinate) clause

The following abbreviations printed above the first vertical
line designate a particular kind of dependent clause, e.g.,

noun = noun clause (He claimed **that he rode on the bus.**)

adj. = adjective clause (The man **who rode on the bus** was
pleased.)

adv. = adverb clause (He was late **because he rode on the
bus.**)

noun
┐‾‾‾‾‾‾‾‾‾‾‾┼‾‾‾‾‾‾‾‾‾‾‾ = dependent (subordinate) noun clause

For further explanation, consult the following terms in
the GLOSSARY OF GRAMMATICAL TERMS at the back of the
book: **independent clause, dependent clause, adjective
clause, adverb clause, noun clause, complex sentence,
compound sentence, gerund, infinitive, participle, verbal, verbal phrase, noun phrase, verb phrase, finite verb,
auxiliary verb, predicate verb, relative pronoun, subordinating conjunction.**

FORMAT OF
MANUSCRIPT

In preparing the final draft of a manuscript, follow the specific directions about format given by your instructor or editor. However, if no specific directions are given, you can be confident that the format of your manuscript will be acceptable if you observe the following conventions:

10 Write on one side of the paper only.

11 Double-space the lines of prose, whether you handwrite or typewrite.

A manuscript submitted to an editor for consideration must be typewritten and double-spaced.

12 Preserve a left-hand and a right-hand margin.

13 Put the title of your paper at the top of the first page of your manuscript—even though you may have put the title on a cover sheet.

See the end of **84** for instructions about how to set down the title of your paper.

14 Number all pages, except the first one (which is never numbered), at the top of the page—in the middle or at the right-hand margin.

15 Secure your manuscript with a paper clip.

Many editors will not even read a manuscript that is stapled together.

16 Use the proper kind of paper.

If you typewrite your manuscript, use white, unlined, opaque paper. If you handwrite your manuscript, use white, lined theme paper.

GRAMMAR

Grammar may be defined as the study of how a language "works"—a study of how the structural system of a language combines with a vocabulary to convey meaning. When we study a foreign language in school, we must study both **vocabulary** and **grammar**, and until we can put the two together, we cannot translate the language. Sometimes we know the meaning of every word in a foreign-language sentence, and yet we cannot translate the sentence because we cannot figure out its grammar. On the other hand, we sometimes can figure out the grammar of the foreign-language sentence, but because we do not know the meaning of one or more words in the sentence, we still cannot translate the sentence.

If you heard or read this sequence of words, you might notice that the sequence bears a marked resemblance to an English sentence:

> The porturbs in the brigger torms have tanted the makrets' rotment brokly.

Although many words in that sequence would be unfamiliar, you would detect that the sequence had the structure of the kind of English sentence that makes a statement, and you might further surmise that this kind of statement pattern was one that said that *porturbs* (whoever they are) had

5

done something to *rotment* (whatever that is), or, to put it another way, that *porturbs* was the subject of the sentence, that *have tanted* was the predicate verb, and that *rotment* was the object of that verb, the receiver of the action performed by the doer, *porturbs*. How were you able to make that much "sense" out of that sequence of strange words? You were able to detect that much sense by noting the following structural signals:

- **Function words**:
  The three occurrences of the article **the**, the preposition **in**, and the auxiliary verb **have**.

- **Inflections and affixes**:
  The **-s** added to nouns to form the plural, the **-er** added to adjectives to form the comparative degree, the **-ed** added to verbs to form the past tense or the past participle, the **-s'** added to nouns to form the plural possessive case, the affix **-ment** added to certain words to form an abstract noun, and the **-ly** added to adjectives to form adverbs.

- **Word order**:
  The basic pattern of a statement or declarative sentence in English is S (subject) + V (verb) + C (complement) or NP (noun phrase) + VP (verb phrase). In the sequence, **The porturbs in the brigger torms** appears to be the S or NP part of the sentence and **have tanted the makrets' rotment brokly** the VP part of the sentence (**have tanted** being the V and **the makrets' rotment brokly** being the C).

- **Intonation (stress, pitch, and juncture)**:
  If the sequence were spoken aloud, you would detect that the sequence had the intonational pattern of a declarative sentence in spoken English.

- **Punctuation and mechanics**:

  If the sequence were written (as it is here), you would observe that it began with a capital letter and ended with a period, two typographical devices that signal a statement in written English.

You would be able to read a relational sense or structural meaning into the string of nonsense words simply by observing the grammatical devices of **inflections, function words**, **word order**, and **intonation** (if spoken) or **punctuation** (if written). Now, if you had a dictionary that defined such words as **porturb**, **brig**, **torm**, **tant**, **makret**, **rotment**, and **brok**, you would be able to translate the full meaning of the sentence. But by observing the structural or grammatical devices alone, you could perceive that the sequence of words

  The porturbs in the brigger torms have tanted the makrets' rotment brokly.

exactly matches the structure of an English sentence like this one:

  The citizens in the larger towns have accepted the legislators' commitment enthusiastically.

What you have been concentrating on is the *grammar* of the sentence, and it is in this structural sense that the term *grammar* is used in the section that follows.

This section on grammar deals with those devices of *inflection, function words,* and *word order* that make it possible for written sentences to convey to readers, clearly and unmistakably, a writer's intended meaning. We are not concerned here with *intonation,* because this handbook deals only with the written language. In a later section, we shall consider the fourth grammatical device of written English, *punctuation.*

20   Apostrophe for Possessive

Use an apostrophe for the possessive case of the noun.

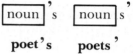

Here are some guidelines for forming the possessive case of the English noun:

(a) As the diagrams above indicate, most English nouns form the possessive case with **'s** (singular) or **s'** (plural). An alternative form of the possessive case consists of an **of** phrase: **the commands of the general** (instead of **the general's commands**).

(b) Nouns that form their plural in ways other than by adding an **s** form their possessive in the plural by adding **'s** to the plural of the noun: **woman's/women's**, **man's/men's**, **child's/children's**, **ox's/oxen's**, **deer's/deer's**, **mouse's/mice's**.

(c) Some writers simply add an apostrophe to form the possessive case of singular nouns ending in **s**:

> the goddess' fame
> the alumnus' contribution
> Keats' odes
> Dickens' novels

However, other writers add the usual **'s** to form the possessive case of such nouns: **goddess's**, **alumnus's** (plural **alumni's**), **Keats's**, **Dickens's**. Take your choice, but be consistent.

(d) The rules for forming the possessive case of pairs of nouns are as follows: (1) in the case of *joint* possession, add **'s** only to the second member of the pair: **John and Mary's mother, the brother and sister's car**, and (2) in the case of *individual* possession, add **'s** to each member of the pair: **the boy's and girl's bedrooms, John's and Mary's tennis rackets, the men's and women's locker rooms**.

21

(e) Form the possessive case of group nouns or compound nouns by adding **'s** to the end of the unit: **commander in chief's, someone else's, president-elect's, editor in chief's, son-in-law's**. In the case of those compounds that form their plural by adding **s** to the first word, form the plural possessive case by adding **'s** to the end of the unit: **editors in chief's, sons-in-law's**.

(f) Normally the **'s** or **s'** is reserved for the possessive case of nouns naming animate creatures (human beings and animals). The **of** phrase is commonly used for the possessive case of inanimate nouns: not **the house's roof** but **the roof of the house**. Usage, however, now sanctions the use of **'s** with some inanimate nouns: **a day's wages, a week's work, the year's death toll, the school's policies, the car's performance, the radio's tone**.

21   Possessive Pronoun *its*

Its is the possessive case of the pronoun it; it's is the contraction of it is or it has.

More mistakes have been made with the pronoun **it** than with any other single word in the English language. The mistakes result from confusion about the two **s** forms of this pronoun. **It's** is often used where **its** is the correct form (**The dog broke it's leg** instead of the correct form, **The dog broke its leg**), and **its** is often used where **it's** is the correct form (**Its a shame that the girl broke her leg** instead of the correct form, **It's a shame that the girl broke her leg**).

If you use **it's** for the possessive case of **it**, you are probably influenced by the **'s** that is used to form the possessive case of the singular noun (**man's hat**). You might be helped to avoid this mistake if you were reminded that *none of the personal pronouns uses* **'s** *to form its possessive case:* **I/my, you/your, he/his, she/her, it/its, we/our, they/their**. So you should write, **The company lost its lease**.

You might also be helped to avoid this mistake if you would remember that the apostrophe has another function in written English: to indicate the omission of one or more letters in an English word, as in contractions (**I'll, don't, she'd**). The apostrophe in the word **it's** signals the contraction of the expression **it is** or **it has**. So you should write, **It's the first loss that the company has suffered** or **It's come to my attention that you are frequently late**.

Don't let this little word defeat you. Get **it** right, once and for all.

22   Subject/Verb Agreement

The predicate verb should agree in number with its subject.

22

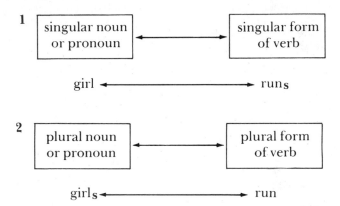

1
| singular noun or pronoun | ⟷ | singular form of verb |

girl ⟷ run**s**

2
| plural noun or pronoun | ⟷ | plural form of verb |

girl**s** ⟷ run

Some typical examples of faulty agreement:

1. He **don't care** about anything.

rewrite:

> He **doesn't care** about anything.

2. The lawyer and the client **agrees** on a fee.

rewrite:

> The lawyer and the client **agree** on a fee.

3. If any one of the substations **are knocked out**, we can resort to reserve stations.

rewrite:

> If any one of the substations **is knocked out**, we can resort to reserve stations.

4. The class **has taken** their seats.

rewrite:

> The class **have taken** their seats.

5. He finds it impossible to live with the ignorance, injustice, poverty, and prejudice that **surrounds** him.

rewrite:

He finds it impossible to live with the ignorance, injustice, poverty, and prejudice that **surround** him.

22

6. Neither the gambler nor Jake **are** really bitter about the run of bad luck or **blame** anyone for the heavy losses.

rewrite:

Neither the gambler nor Jake **is** really bitter about the run of bad luck or **blames** anyone for the heavy losses.

Expressions like **He don't care about anything** are not so much "mistakes" in agreement as carry-overs from the dialect that people speak, quite acceptably, in their own communities. Writers should be aware of the standard form of the verb in written prose: **He doesn't care about anything** (a singular verb with a singular subject).

Most errors of agreement in written prose are the result of carelessness, inadvertence, or uncertainty. The writer often knows better but merely slips up. Errors in agreement often occur when several words intervene between the simple subject of the sentence and the predicate verb, as in sentence **3**: **If any one of the substations are knocked out**. . . . The simple subject of the **if** clause here is **one**, but because the plural noun **substations** (the object of the preposition **of**) intervened between that singular subject and the verb, the writer was influenced to use the plural form of the verb (**are knocked out**) instead of the correct singular form (**is knocked out**). Careful proofreading will often catch such inadvertent errors of agreement.

Errors due to uncertainty are another matter. Uncertainty about whether the verb should be singular or plural arises in cases where (1) the subject is compound, (2) the subject is a collective noun, (3) the subject of the sentence follows the structure **there is/there are**, and (4) the subject takes the form of a special structure, such as **one of those who** or **this man as well as**. Here are some guidelines for these puzzling cases:

(a) Compound subject

22

(1) Singular subjects joined by **and** usually take a plural verb.

John and his sister **were questioned** by the police.

(2) Singular subjects joined by **or** or by the correlative conjunctions **either . . . or**, **neither . . . nor** take a singular verb.

John or his sister **runs** the store during the week.

Neither the nurse nor Dr. Bruce **is** worried about the patient's condition.

(3) When both subjects are plural, the verb is plural.

The detectives and the insurance agents **have expressed** their belief in the innocence of the brother and sister.

Neither the detectives nor the insurance agents **have expressed** any doubts about the innocence of the brother and sister.

(4) When one subject is singular and the other subject is plural and the subjects are joined by **or** or by the correlative conjunctions **either . . . or**, **neither . . . nor**, the verb agrees in number with the closer subject.

Either John or his parents work in the store on Sunday.

Neither the brothers nor the sister **appears** to be cooperative.

However, plural or singular subjects joined by the correlative conjunctions **both . . . and** or **not only . . . but** (**also**) take a plural verb.

Both John and his sister **have agreed** to cooperate with the police.

Not only the brother but also the sister **appear** to be cooperative.

(b) Collective noun as subject

(1) If the collective noun is considered as a **group**, the verb is singular.

The jury **has made up** its mind.

The committee **was elected** unanimously.

The number of students who failed **has increased** by 50 percent.

(2) If the collective noun is considered as **individuals**, each acting on his or her own, the verb is plural.

The jury **have made up** their minds.

The committee **wish** to offer their congratulations to the new chairperson.

A number of students **have asked** the dean for an extension.

(c) The structure **there is/are, there was/were**

(1) If the delayed or real subject following **there** is singular, the verb is singular.

There **is** a remarkable consensus among the committee members.

(2) If the delayed or real subject following **there** is plural, the verb is plural.

There **were** ten dissenting votes from the stockholders.

(d) Special structures

(1) In the structure **one of the** [plural nouns—e.g., *women*] **who**, the predicate verb of the **who** clause is plural because the antecedent of the subject **who** is the plural noun rather than the singular **one**.

Matilda is one of the women who **refuse** to accept the ruling.

*(here the antecedent of **who** is the plural noun **women**)*

(2) Exception: if **the only** precedes **one of the** [plural noun—e.g., women] **who**, the predicate verb of the **who** clause is singular, because the subject **who** in that case refers to the singular **one** rather than to the plural object of the preposition **of**.

22

Matilda is the only one of the women who **refuses** to accept the ruling.

(3) A singular subject followed by structures like **as well as**, **in addition to**, **together with** takes a singular verb.

(A plural subject, of course, followed by any of these structures, would take a plural verb. See the third example below.)

The sergeant as well as his superior officers **praises** his platoon.

Linda Myers along with her roommate **has denied** the charges.

The students together with their counselor **deny** that there has been any distribution of drugs in the dorms.

(4) Nouns that do not end in *s* but that are plural in meaning take a plural verb.

The bacteria **require** constant attention.

These data **are** consistent with the judge's findings.

The deer **are running** loose in the state park.

(5) Nouns that end in *s* but that are singular in meaning take a singular verb.

My grandmother's scissors **was** very dull.

Ten dollars **is** a fair price for the coat.

Two weeks **seems** a long time when you are waiting for someone you love.

(6) Noun clauses serving as the subject of the sentence always take a singular verb.

That Sara decided to go to college **pleases** me very much.

What caused the accident **was** two stones in the road.

(7) In inverted structures, where the subject follows the verb, a singular subject takes a singular verb, and a plural subject takes a plural verb.

At each checkpoint **stands** a heavily armed soldier.

Happy **were** they to see us arrive.

Among the crew **were** Carson, Barton, and Farmon.

23 Noun/Pronoun Agreement

A pronoun must agree in person, number, and gender with its antecedent noun.

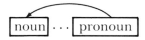

Examples of faulty agreement between a pronoun and its antecedent:

1. A **family** cannot go camping these days without a truckload of gadgets to make **your** campsite look like home.

rewrite:

   A **family** cannot go camping these days without a truckload of gadgets to make **their** campsite look like home.

2. The women threw some unsinkable **items** overboard for the sailor, even though she knew **it** would probably not save him.

rewrite:

> The woman threw some unsinkable **items** overboard for the sailor, even though she knew **they** would probably not save him.

3. The old **car** did **her** best to make the steep hill.

rewrite:

> The old **car** did **its** best to make the steep hill.

4. Each **student** should bring **his** schedule cards to the bursar's office.

rewrite:

> **Students** should bring **their** schedule cards to the bursar's office.

Pronouns, which are substitutes for nouns, share the following features with nouns: **number** (singular or plural) and **gender** (masculine or feminine or neuter). What nouns and pronouns do not share in common is the full range of **person**. All nouns are **third person** exclusively; but some pronouns are **first person** (**I, we**), some are **second person** (**you**), and some are **third person** (**he, she, it, they, one, some, none, all, everybody**).

A firm grammatical principle is that a pronoun must correspond with whatever features of person, number, and gender it has in common with its antecedent noun. A second-person pronoun (*you*) should not be linked with a third-person noun (*family*) (see sentence **1**). A singular pronoun (*it*) should not be linked with a plural noun (*items*) (see sentence **2**). A feminine pronoun (*her*) should not be linked with a neuter noun (*car*) (see sentence **3**).

Sentence **4** is not so much an instance of faulty agreement as it is an instance of *inappropriate* agreement. The problem in that example stems from the fact that the English language has no convenient pronoun for indicating masculine-or-feminine gender. It has been a common practice in the past to use the generic **he** (**him, his**) to refer to nouns of common gender like **student**, **teacher**, **writer**, **candidate**, **driver**. In recent years, however, the use of generic **he** and its derivative forms (**his**, **him**) to refer to singular nouns that could be either masculine or feminine has been considered an example of the sexist bias of the English language. Many writers today are making a genuine effort to avoid offending readers with any kind of sexist language.

How do you deal with the agreement problem exhibited in sentence 4? One way is for you to resort to the use of an admittedly awkward pronoun form like **his or her**, **his/her**, or **his** (**her**), as in the following sentence: "The **student** should bring **his or her** schedule cards to the bursar's office." Another way is to use a plural noun wherever possible: "**Students** should bring **their** schedule cards to the bursar's office." In some cases, it is possible to reword the sentence so that no pronoun has to be used, as in this revision: "The **student** should bring all schedule cards to the bursar's office."

Mismatchings of nouns and pronouns in person and gender are not very common in written prose. Most mismatchings of nouns and pronouns involve number—a singular pronoun referring to a plural noun (**items . . . it**, as in sentence 2) or a plural pronoun referring to a singular noun (**student . . . their**). Another agreement problem derives from the ambiguity of number of such pronouns as **everyone**, **everybody**, **all**, **none**, **some**, **each**. Although there are exceptions, the following guidelines are generally reliable:

(a) **Everyone**, **everybody**, **anybody**, **anyone** invariably take singular verbs and, in formal usage at least, should be referred to by a singular pronoun.

Everyone brings **his or her** schedule cards to the bursar's office.

Anybody who wants to run in the race has to pay **her** entry fee by Friday.

(b) All and **some** are singular or plural according to the context. If the **of** phrase following the pronoun specifies a *mass* or a *bulk* of something, the pronoun is singular. If the **of** phrase specifies a *number* of things or persons, the pronoun is plural.

23

Some of the fabric lost **its** coloring.

All of the sugar was spoiled by **its** own chemical imbalance.

Some of the students complained about **their** dormitory rooms.

All of the women registered **their** protests at City Hall.

(c) None is singular or plural according to the context. (The distinction in particular cases is sometimes so subtle that a writer could justify either a singular or a plural pronoun.)

None of the young men **was** willing to turn in **his** driver's license. (*but* **were** . . . **their** *could also be justified in this case*)

None of the young men **were** as tall as **their** fathers. (*here it would be harder to justify the singular forms* **was** . . . **his**)

(d) Each is singular.

Each of them declared **her** allegiance to democracy.

(e) For guidelines about the **number** of collective nouns (like *family* in sentence **1**), see **(b)** in the previous section **(22)**.

If you match up your pronouns in person, number, and gender with their antecedent nouns, you will make it easier for your reader to figure out what the pronouns refer to.

24 Pronoun Antecedent

A pronoun should have a clear antecedent.

24

?.... | pronoun |

Examples of no antecedent or an unclear antecedent for the pronoun (an antecedent is a noun in a previous group of words to which a pronoun can refer):

1. Mayor Worthington, acting on the advice of her physician, resigned her office, and the city council, responding to a mandate from the voters, was swift to accept **it**
(what did the council accept?)

rewrite:
Mayor Worthington, acting on the advice of her physician, resigned her office, and the city council, responding to a mandate from the voters, was swift to accept her resignation.

2. John told his father that **his** car wouldn't start.
(whose car? the father's or John's?)

rewrite:
John told his father, "Your car won't start."
or
John told his father, "My car won't start."

3. I decided to break the engagement with my girlfriend, **which** distressed my parents very much.
(just what was it that distressed your parents?)

rewrite:
I decided to break the engagement with my girlfriend, a decision which distressed my parents very much.

4. The league's first major step was to sponsor a cleanup day, but **it** could not enlist enough volunteers.
(a pronoun should not refer to a noun functioning as a possessive or as a modifier—here **league's**)

rewrite:
>   The league took as its first major step the sponsorship of a cleanup day, but it could not enlist enough volunteers.

5. I enjoyed the sun and the sand and the surf, and **this** revealed to me that I really prefer a vacation at the beach.
    (what does **this** refer to?)

rewrite:
>   I enjoyed the sun and the sand and the surf, and this experience revealed to me that I really prefer a vacation at the beach.

24

Careless handling of the pronoun often blocks communication between writer and reader. As the writer, you always know what you meant the pronoun to stand for, but if there is no antecedent (a noun in the previous group of words to which the pronoun can refer) or if it is difficult to find the noun to which the pronoun refers, your reader will not know—and will have to guess—what the pronoun stands for.

Whenever you use a pronoun, check to see whether there is a noun in the previous group of words that could be put in the place of the pronoun. Let us apply this test to sentence 1. There are three neuter, singular nouns to which the final pronoun **it** could refer: **advice**, **office**, **mandate**. But when we put each of these nouns, successively, in the place of **it**, we see that none of them names what the council accepted. If we pondered the sentence long enough, we might eventually figure out that what the council accepted was the mayor's *resignation*. But since the noun *resignation* appears nowhere in the sentence, we must use the noun phrase **her resignation** instead of the pronoun **it**.

Sentence 2 is an example of an unclear antecedent. The pronoun reference is unclear because the pronoun **his** is ambiguous—that is, there are two nouns to which the mas-

24

culine, singular pronoun **his** could refer: **John** and **father**. So we cannot tell whether it was the father's car or John's car that wouldn't start. If the context in which that sentence occurred did not help us determine whose car was being referred to, we could avoid the ambiguity by turning the sentence into a direct quotation: either **John told his father, "Your car won't start"** or **John told his father, "My car won't start."**

Although the use of the pronoun **this** or **that** to refer to a whole idea in a previous clause or sentence has long been a common practice in spoken English, you should be aware that by using the demonstrative pronoun **this** or **that** to refer to a whole idea in the previous clause or sentence, you run the risk that the reference of the pronoun will be vague or ambiguous for your readers. If you do not want to run that risk, you can use **this** or **that** (or the corresponding plural, **these** or **those**) as an adjective instead of as a pronoun. The adjective would go before some noun summing up what **this** or **that** stands for. In sentence **5**, we can avoid the vague pronoun reference by using the phrase **this experience** instead of the pronoun **this**.

The use of the relative pronoun **which** or **that** to refer to a whole idea in the main clause rather than to a specific noun in that clause is also becoming more common. But there is a risk in this use similar to the one that attends the use of **this** or **that** to refer to a whole idea. We can save the reader from being even momentarily baffled by the **which** in sentence **3** by supplying a summary noun to serve as the antecedent for that relative pronoun. In revising sentence **3**, we have put the noun **decision** before the pronoun **which**.

The problem with the pronoun reference in sentence **4**

stems from the linguistic fact that a pronoun does not readily reveal its antecedent if it refers to a noun that is functioning in a subordinate structure such as a possessive (the **school's** principal), a modifier of a noun (the **school** term), or an object of a preposition (in the **school**). One remedy for the vague pronoun reference in sentence **4** is to use the noun **league** rather than the pronoun **it**: ". . . but the **league** could not enlist enough volunteers." Another remedy is the one we used in rewriting sentence **4**: making **league** the subject of the first clause so that the **it** in the second clause would have an antecedent.

25   Dangling Modifier

An introductory verbal or verbal phrase must find its "doer" in the subject of the main clause.

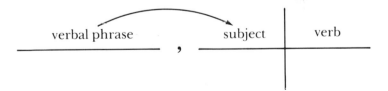

Examples of "dangling" verbal phrases:

1. Revolving at a rate of 2200 revolutions per minute, the janitor turned off the overheated generator.

rewrite:
   Revolving at the rate of 2200 revolutions per minute, the overheated generator was turned off by the janitor.

or

The janitor turned off the overheated generator, which was revolving at a rate of 2200 revolutions per minute.

2. By stressing positive action, her inferiority complex can be overcome.

rewrite:

By stressing positive action, she can overcome her inferiority complex.

3. Refusing to be inducted into the army, the World Boxing Association stripped Muhammad Ali of his title.

rewrite:

Refusing to be inducted into the army, Muhammad Ali was stripped of his title by the World Boxing Association.

or

The World Boxing Association stripped Muhammad Ali of his title for refusing to be inducted into the army.

4. In order to pass examinations, it is necessary for us to study diligently.

rewrite:

In order to pass examinations, we must study diligently.

or

It is necessary for us to study diligently in order to pass examinations.

In English, an introductory verbal phrase (dominated by a participle, a gerund, or an infinitive) naturally adheres to the subject of the main clause. When the subject of the main clause is not the "doer" of the action indicated in the verbal, we say that the verbal **dangles**—that it is not attached to the proper agent. In each of the sample sentences, the subject of the main clause is not the "doer" of the action specified by the introductory verbal (**revolving**, **stressing**, **refusing**, **to pass**).

Sometimes in revising our sentence to make the subject of the main clause the doer of the action specified in our introductory verbal, we have to resort to a rather awkward passive verb, as we did in revisions **1** and **3** above. In such cases, we may decide to recast the sentence so that it doesn't begin with a verbal phrase. If we start our sentence with a verbal phrase, we cannot start the main clause of that sentence with a structure like **there is** or **it is** (see sentence **4**).

To prevent dangling verbals, writers should always make sure that the subject of the main clause is the doer of the action specified in the preceding verbal.

26 Misplaced Modifier

Misplaced modifiers lead to a misreading of the sentence.

Examples of misplaced modifiers:

1. Anyone who reads a newspaper **frequently** will notice that many people are now concerned about pollution.

rewrite:
    Anyone who frequently reads a newspaper will notice that many people are now concerned about pollution.
or
    Anyone who reads a newspaper will notice frequently that many people are now concerned about pollution.

2. He has **only** a face that a mother could love.

rewrite:

He has a face that only a mother could love.

3. Felicity **even** smiles when she is sleeping.

rewrite:

Felicity smiles even when she is sleeping.

4. The judge explained why traffic violations are a menace to society **on Tuesday**.

rewrite:

The judge explained on Tuesday why traffic violations are a menace to society.

5. **After you entered** the park, the sponsors of the Summerfest decided that you would not have to spend any more money at the concession stands.

rewrite:

The sponsors of the Summerfest decided that after you entered the park, you would not have to spend any more money at the concession stands.

6. She paid five dollars for a dress at the county fair **that she despised**.

rewrite:

At the county fair, she paid five dollars for a dress that she despised.

Because English is a language that depends heavily on word order to protect meaning, related words, phrases, and clauses should be placed as close as possible to one another. Adverbial and adjectival modifiers especially must be placed as close as possible to words that they modify. Failure to juxtapose related words, phrases, or clauses may lead to a misreading—that is, to a reading different from what the author intended.

In sentence **1**, we have an example of what is called a **squinting modifier**, a modifier that looks in two directions at once. In that sentence, the adverb **frequently** sits between two verbs that it could modify—**reads** and **will notice**. If the writer intends the adverb to modify the act of *reading* rather than the act of *noticing*, the position of **frequently** should be shifted so that the sentence reads as follows: **Anyone who frequently reads a newspaper will notice that many people are now concerned about pollution**. If, however, the writer intends the adverb to modify the act of *noticing*, **frequently** should be shifted to a position between **will** and **notice** or after **notice**.

Because **only** in sentence **2** is placed in the wrong clause of the sentence, it modifies **a face**. The writer could avoid an unwanted laugh by putting **only** where it belongs: **He has a face that only a mother could love**.

Chances are that the writer of sentence **3** did not intend **even** to modify the act of *smiling*. Shifting **even** will make the sentence say what the writer probably meant it to say: **Felicity smiles even when she is sleeping.**

Because the prepositional phrase **on Tuesday** has been put in the wrong place in sentence **4**, it does not modify the word that it should be modifying (**explained**) and therefore does not say what the writer intended to say. The sentence should be revised to read as follows: **The judge explained on Tuesday why traffic violations are a menace to society**.

Notice how shifting the position of the modifying clauses in sentences **5** and **6** makes the sentences say what they were probably intended to say.

Reading sentences aloud will sometimes reveal the misplacement of modifying words, phrases, and clauses.

26

27 Parallelism

Preserve parallel structure by using units of the same grammatical kind.

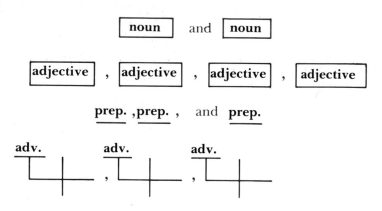

Examples of breakdown in parallelism:

1. The old beliefs about theft have been rejected **as superstitions** and **detrimental** to one's prestige.
   (noun and adjective)

rewrite:

   The old beliefs about theft have been rejected **as superstitious** and **as detrimental** to one's prestige.

2. He was a **miser**, a **bachelor**, and **egotistical**.
   (noun, noun, adjective)

rewrite:

   He was a **miser**, a **bachelor**, and an **egotist**.

3. John was **healthy**, **wealthy**, and an **athlete**.
   (adjective, adjective, noun)

rewrite:

   John was **healthy**, **wealthy**, and **athletic**.

4. First of all, Daisy was an **adult, married**, and **had a young daughter**.

(noun, adjective, verb phrase)

rewrite:

First of all, Daisy was an **adult**, a **married woman**, and the **mother of a young daughter**.

5. Lincoln was a man **of the people, for the people**, and **loved by the people**.

(prepositional phrase, prepositional phrase, participial phrase)

rewrite:

Lincoln was a man **who was born of the people, who worked for the people**, and **who was loved by the people**.

6. The president commended the steelworkers **for their patriotism** and **because they did not ask for a wage increase**.

(prepositional phrase, adverb clause)

rewrite:

The president commended the steelworkers **for their patriotism** and **for their restraint**.

7. I read **for personal enlightenment** and **to develop mental sharpness**.

(prepositional phrase, infinitive phrase)

rewrite:

I read **to gain personal enlightenment** and **to develop mental sharpness**.

8. The advertisers **not only** convince the reader that the Continental is a luxury car **but also** that the car confers status on its owner.

(violation of parallelism with correlative conjunctions)

rewrite:

The advertisers convince the reader not only **that the Continental is a luxury car** but also **that the car confers status on its owner**.

The principle governing parallel structure is that a pair or a series (three or more) of units serving the same function in a sentence should be composed of similar elements—e.g., nouns with nouns, adjectives with adjectives, not a mixture of nouns and adjectives. A breakdown in parallelism wrenches coherence because it disrupts the expectation that when a series starts out with one kind of element, it will stay with that element.

The obvious way to correct a breakdown in parallelism is to convert all the members of the pair or the series to units of the same structure or part of speech. In converting all the members of a pair or a series to units of the same structure or part of speech, we sometimes have an either/or choice available, but usually one of the options will be stylistically preferable to the other. In revising sentences **2**, **6**, and **7**, we could have taken another option:

2. He was **miserly**, **single**, and **egotistical**.

6. The president commended the steelworkers **because they were patriotic** and **because they did not ask for a wage increase**.

7. I read simply **for personal enlightenment** and **for the development of mental sharpness**.

Whenever alternative ways of repairing the breakdown in parallelism are available, we have to exercise judgment in deciding which is the better stylistic choice in a particular case.

Sentences **1**, **3**, and **4**, however, do not readily lend themselves to alternative revisions. In sentence **1**, for instance, the writer could convert the pair to two nouns (**superstitions** and **detriments**), but that wording is not as stylistically satisfactory as the conversion to two adjectives (**superstitious** and **detrimental**). The predicate terms in sentence **3** cannot be converted to three nouns because there are no single-word noun equivalents of the adjectives **healthy** and **wealthy**; so this sentence can be made parallel only by turning all three units into adjectives. The use of nouns or noun phrases was the only option available for the revision of sentence **4** because there is no noun or adjective equivalent of the verb phrase **had a young daughter**.

Correcting the violation of parallelism in sentence **5** was almost impossible because of the unavailability of three equivalent prepositional phrases or three equivalent participial phrases. The best that could be done in that case was to use three **who** clauses, but although that revision makes the sentence grammatically parallel, it is not stylistically satisfactory.

Sentence **8** illustrates a violation of parallelism when correlative conjunctions are used: **either** . . . **or**; **neither** . . . **nor**; **not (only)** . . . **but (also)**. The principle operating with correlative conjunctions is that the same grammatical structure must be on the right-hand side of both conjunctions. We can more easily see the breakdown in parallelism if we lay out sentence **8** in two layers:

> The advertisers **not only** convince the reader that the Continental is a luxury car
>
> > **but also** that the car confers status on its owner.

On the right-hand side of **not only**, there is this grammatical sequence: a verb (**convince**), a noun (**the reader**), and a noun clause (**that the Continental is a luxury car**). On the right-hand side of **but also**, however, there is *only* the noun clause (**that the car confers status on its owner**). The faulty parallelism can be revised in either of two ways:

> The advertisers **not only** convince the reader that the Continental is a luxury car
>
> > **but also** convince the reader that the car confers status on its owner.

The advertisers convince the reader **not only** that the Continental is a luxury car

but also that the car confers status on its owner.

In both revisions, we now have the same grammatical structures on the right-hand side of both correlative conjunctions. But because the second revision has fewer words and less repetition than the first one, it is probably the better of the two revisions.

Note how parallelism is preserved in the following two sentences using correlative conjunctions:

Either he will love the one and hate the other, **or** he will hate the one and love the other.

He will **either** love the one and hate the other **or** hate the one and love the other.

The principle governing parallelism: **like must be joined with like.**

28 Subordinate Conjunction *that*

Use the subordinate conjunction *that* if it will prevent a possible misreading.

Examples where it would be advisable to insert **that**:

1. My father believed ⋏ his doctor, who was a boyhood friend, was wholly trustworthy.

rewrite:

My father believed **that** his doctor, who was a boyhood friend, was wholly trustworthy.

2. A more realistic person would probably assert ⋏ these statements about the ad were frivolous and sentimental.

rewrite:

A more realistic person would probably assert **that** these statements about the ad were frivolous and sentimental.

3. He discovered ∧ the radio and the tape recorder in his roommate's closet had been stolen.

rewrite:

He discovered **that** the radio and the tape recorder in his roommate's closet had been stolen.

4. The author reported ∧ as soon as a Jew became intensely depressed in camp and lost all purpose for living, death came shortly after.

rewrite:

The author reported **that** as soon as a Jew became intensely depressed in camp and lost all purpose for living, death came shortly after.

5. Professor Clements maintained ∧ communism rejected capitalism and ∧ democracy rejected collective ownership.

rewrite:

Professor Clements maintained **that** communism rejected capitalism and **that** democracy rejected collective ownership.

The tendency of our language is toward economy of means. So we omit syllables in such contractions as **he's**, **she'll**, **we'd**, **won't**, and we resort to such common elliptical expressions as **not all [of] the men**; **she is taller than I [am tall]**; **when [I was] in the fourth grade, I went to the zoo with my mother**. We also frequently omit the conjunction **that**, which introduces a noun clause serving as the object of a verb, as in "He said [**that**] he was going" and "He announced [**that**] I was a candidate for office."

Whether to use the conjunction **that** in written prose will be a problem only when a noun clause is being used as the direct object of a verb—but not in every instance of such use. If there is no chance that a sentence will be misread, it is all right, even in written prose, to omit **that**. But if there is a chance that a noun phrase following the verb may be read as the object of the verb rather than as the subject of the subsequent clause, then we can prevent even a momentary misreading by inserting **that** at the beginning of the noun clause. What follows may make all of this discussion clearer.

In a sentence like "He believed they were going," it is safe to omit **that** after **believed** because **they** cannot possibly be read as the object of **believed**. (If **they** were the object of the verb here, the pronoun would have to be **them—He believed them**.) But in a sentence like **1**, it is not only possible but likely that the noun phrase **his doctor** will initially be read as the object of **believed** (**he believed his doctor**). Of course, as soon as we come to the predicate **was wholly trustworthy**, we realize that we have misread the sentence, and so we have to back up and reread the sentence as the writer intended it to be read. But the writer could have prevented that initial misreading by inserting **that** after **believed—My father believed that his doctor, who was a boyhood friend, was wholly trustworthy**. Then the sentence can be read in only one way—the way in which the writer intended it to be read.

Read the other sample sentences aloud, the first time omitting **that**, the second time inserting **that** where the (∧) is. By doing this double reading of the sentences aloud, you will notice how the insertion of **that** ensures that the sentences will be read in the way the writer intended them to be read.

When a reader has to reread a sentence in order to make sense of it, the writer is often the one to blame. Inserting **that** where it is necessary or advisable is one way to spare readers from having to reread a sentence.

29   Sentence Fragment

Avoid the careless or indefensible use of sentence fragments.

29

——————— .

Examples of questionable sentence fragments:

1. They tried to explain to the police that they intended to drive the brakeless car only two blocks to the repair shop. **Although they soon became aware that neither of the police officers was paying any attention to their explanation**.

rewrite:
   They tried to explain to the police that they intended to drive the brakeless car only two blocks to the repair shop, although they soon became aware that neither of the police officers was paying any attention to their explanation.

2. **The reason for Holden's disappointment being that his sister wasn't there to comfort him**.

rewrite:
   The reason for Holden's disappointment was that his sister wasn't there to comfort him.

3. Both men are alike in that they try to help people if the effort does not result in too much trouble for themselves. **Herenger, in his idea that it is good to help someone with "so little trouble to himself," and the Baron**, who believes in giving money to someone as long as there is no further responsibility involved.

rewrite:
   Both men are alike in that they try to help people if the effort does not result in too much trouble for themselves. Herenger believes that it is good to help someone with "so little trouble to himself," and the Baron believes in giving money to someone as long as there is no further responsibility involved.

4. The bond between Gretta and Michael was strong enough to make him face death rather than be separated from her. **The tragedy here that such a love could not be consummated and that one so young should be cut off just at the dawn of his life**.

rewrite:

The bond between Gretta and Michael was strong enough to make him face death rather than be separated from her. The tragedy here was that such a love could not be consummated and that one so young should be cut off just at the dawn of life.

5. I know what you're thinking. **The wife trying to maintain her stubborn pride, the husband feeling guilty and remorseful, the children looking desperately for somebody to reconcile their parents**.

rewrite:

I know what you're thinking. You're thinking that the wife is trying to maintain her stubborn pride, that the husband is feeling guilty and remorseful, and that the children are looking desperately for somebody to reconcile their parents.

A sentence fragment can be defined as a string of words, between an initial capital letter and a period or a question mark, that lacks a subject or a finite-verb predicate (or both) or that has a subject and a finite-verb predicate but is made part of a larger structure by a relative pronoun (**who**, **which**, **that**) or by a subordinating conjunction (**although**, **because**, **if**, **when**, and so on).

In example **1**, the string of words beginning with **although** and terminating with a period is a sentence fragment because even though it has a subject (**they**) and a finite-verb predicate (**became**), it is turned into a dependent clause by the subordinating conjunction **although**. If instead of using the subordinating conjunction **although**, the writer had used a coordinating conjunction (**but**) or a conjunctive adverb (**however**), the words that follow would be a complete sentence. If **although** is used to begin that string of words, however, those words must be made a part of the preceding independent clause.

Example **2** is a sentence fragment because there is no finite-verb predicate for the noun **reason**. (There is a finite verb in the string—**wasn't**—but that verb is the predicate of the dependent noun clause **that his sister wasn't there to comfort him**.) There is a verbal here (the participle **being**), but by itself, that participle cannot serve as the predicate for **reason**. The simplest way to make that fragment a complete sentence is to convert the participle **being** into the finite verb **was**.

The boldface string of words in example **3** is a sentence fragment because neither **Herenger** nor **Baron**, both of which appear to be "subjects," has a predicate verb. By supplying the finite verb **believes** for both subjects, we converted that fragment into a compound sentence consisting of two independent clauses.

Apparently, the author of example **4** left out the verb in the boldface string of words, owing to mere carelessness. If the author had read the string aloud, he or she probably would have noticed that the predicate verb was missing. Putting in a verb like **was** will correct that sentence fragment.

Because example **5** lacks a predicate verb in the boldfaced string of words, it is difficult—if not impossible—for us to see what the relationship between the two groups of words is and therefore what the author is trying to say. Because we do not know what the author meant, we can only suggest possible revisions. The revision above is only one of a number of ways of rewriting the strings in order to eliminate the sentence fragment.

Whether a string of words constitutes a complete sentence or only a sentence fragment is a grammatical con-

29

cern; whether the use of a sentence fragment is appropriate in a particular context and is therefore justifiable is a rhetorical or stylistic concern. It is a fact of life that we sometimes communicate with one another in sentence fragments. Note for instance the following exchange:

29

> Where are you going tonight?
> The movies.
> Who with?
> Jack.
> Where?
> The Palace.
> What time?
> About 8:30.
> By car?
> No, by bus.
> Can I go?
> Sure.

Once the context of that dialogue was established, both speakers communicated in fragments. Notice, though, that the dialogue had to be initiated by a complete sentence (the question **Where are you going tonight?**) and that later the first speaker had to resort again to a complete sentence (**Can I go?**) because there was no way to phrase that question clearly in a fragmentary way.

Native speakers of a language can converse in fragments because each of them is capable of mentally supplying what is missing from an utterance. When in response to the initial question the second speaker answers, **The movies**, that phrase conveys a meaning because the first speaker is able to supply, mentally and perhaps subconsciously, the missing elements in the fragmentary reply: (**I am going to**) **the movies**.

All of us have encountered sentence fragments in the written prose of some very reputable writers. Predicateless sentences are most likely to be found in mood-setting descriptive and narrative prose, as in this first paragraph of Charles Dickens's novel *Bleak House:*

29

> London, Michaelmas Term lately over, and the Lord Chancellor sitting in Lincoln's Inn Hall. Implacable November weather. As much mud in the streets, as if the waters had but newly retired from the face of the earth, and it would not be wonderful to meet a Megalosaurus, forty feet long or so, waddling like an elephantine lizard up Holborn Hill. Smoke lowering down from chimney-pots, making a soft black drizzle, with flakes of soot in it as big as full-grown snow-flakes—gone into mourning, one might imagine, for the death of the sun. Dogs, undistinguishable in mire. Horses, scarcely better; splashed to their blinkers. Foot passengers, jostling one another's umbrellas, in a general infection of illtemper, and losing their foothold at street-corners, where tens of thousands of other foot passengers have been slipping and sliding since the day broke (if this day ever broke), adding new deposits to the crust upon crust of mud, sticking at those points tenaciously to the pavement and accumulating at compound interest.

In that paragraph, there are a few clauses (that is, groups of words with a subject and a finite-verb predicate), but the paragraph consists primarily of nouns and noun phrases, some of them modified by participial phrases (e.g., **sitting in Lincoln's Inn Hall**, **splashed to their blinkers**, **jostling one another's umbrellas**). (It might be a good exercise for you to go through the paragraph and see if you can distinguish the sentence fragments from the complete sentences.) Although the passage is largely lacking in statements made with finite verbs, the sequence of sentence fragments does create effects that Dickens could not have achieved—or achieved as well—with complete sentences.

The points to be made in citing these examples of spoken and written discourse are (1) that sentence fragments are a part of the English language (in that sense, they are "grammatical"), (2) that in certain contexts they do communicate meaning, and (3) that in some circumstances and for some purposes they are appropriate and therefore acceptable, effective, and even stylistically desirable. But you should be aware of what you are doing. You should be conscious that you are deliberately using a sentence fragment instead of a complete sentence; otherwise, you will be guilty of a *careless* use of a sentence fragment. And you should have some purpose or effect in mind when you use a sentence fragment; otherwise, you will be guilty of an *indefensible* use of a sentence fragment. In every case, you should be aware of the possibility that the sentence fragment may not communicate clearly with readers.

30 Comma Splice

Independent clauses cannot be spliced simply with a comma.

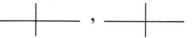

Examples of comma splices:

1. We are not allowed to think for ourselves, that privilege is reserved for administrators.

rewrite:

We are not allowed to think for ourselves; that privilege is reserved for administrators.

2. The biggest government spender, according to *Time* magazine,

is the Department of Agriculture, the next biggest spender is the Department of Defense.

rewrite:
The biggest government spender, according to *Time* magazine, is the Department of Agriculture. The next biggest spender is the Department of Defense.

30

3. Our minds are never challenged by the television set, it is just so much easier to sit there than to read a book.

rewrite:
Our minds are never challenged by the television set, **for** it is so much easier to sit there than to read a book.

4. The members of the city council are convinced of the need for wheelchair lifts on public buses, however, they can't figure out how the city or the bus companies could finance such equipment.

rewrite:
Although the members of the city council are convinced of the need for wheelchair lifts on public buses, they can't figure out how the city or the bus companies could finance such equipment.

A comma splice is the result of joining independent clauses with nothing but a comma. *A comma is a separating device, not a joining device.* A comma splice is, therefore, an error in punctuation, but since punctuation is, for the written language, the grammatical equivalent of vocal intonation in the spoken language, this error in punctuation can also be considered an error in grammar.

Independent clauses must be joined either by a coordinating conjunction (**and**, **but**, **or**, **for**, **nor**, **yet**, **so**) or by a semicolon. In addition to these two ways of properly splicing independent clauses, there are two other ways of fixing up a comma splice: by making separate sentences of the two clauses and by subordinating one of the clauses. Using each of these methods in turn, let us correct the comma splice in the first sample sentence above.

(a) Insert the appropriate coordinating conjunction after the comma:

> We are not allowed to think for ourselves, **for** that privilege is reserved for administrators.

(b) Substitute a semicolon for the comma:

> We are not allowed to think for ourselves; that privilege is reserved for administrators.

(c) Put a period at the end of the first independent clause and begin a new sentence with the first word of the second independent clause:

> We are not allowed to think for ourselves. That privilege is reserved for administrators.

(d) Subordinate one of the independent clauses:

> We are not allowed to think for ourselves, **since** that privilege is reserved for administrators.

Although these four ways of repairing a comma splice are always available, one of them will usually be better in a particular instance. In sentence 1, splicing the two clauses with a semicolon would probably be best: **We are not allowed to think for ourselves; that privilege is reserved for administrators**. The semicolon here effects the closest union of the two related clauses and best points up the irony between the thoughts in the two clauses. We have made our choice of the semicolon on stylistic grounds; grammatically, the other three options are equally correct.

See **66** and **67** in the section on punctuation for the proper use of the semicolon.

31   Fused Sentence or Run-on Sentence

Do not run independent clauses together without a conjunction or the proper punctuation.

Examples of independent clauses run together:

1. Why am I qualified to speak on this subject I just finished three dreadful years of high school.

rewrite:

Why am I qualified to speak on this subject? I just finished three dreadful years of high school.

2. Those shiny red apples sitting on my desk pleased me very much they were tokens of affection from my pupils.

rewrite:

Those shiny red apples sitting on my desk pleased me very much, **for** they were tokens of affection from my students.

3. Two suspects were arrested last week one of them was a woman.

rewrite:

Two suspects were arrested last week; one of them was a woman.

4. Leggatt was blackballed for having killed a man thus he would never be able to work on a ship again.

rewrite:

Because Leggatt was blackballed for having killed a man, he would never be able to work on a ship again.

The term commonly used to label two or more independent clauses that have been run together without any conjunction or punctuation is **fused sentence** or **run-on sentence**. Fused sentences are not as common in writing as comma splices; but when they occur, they are even more of a stumbling block for a reader than comma splices are. If the writers of the sample sentences above had read their strings of words aloud, they would have detected a natural stopping place—a place where the expression of one thought ended and the expression of another began.

31

Once the writers had detected the fused sentence, they could then consider how best to revise it. Fused sentences can be corrected in the same four ways that comma splices can be corrected:

(a) Join the independent clauses with the appropriate co-ordinating conjunction (see revision of **2** above).

(b) Splice the independent clauses with a semicolon (see the revision of **3** above).

(c) Make separate sentences of the independent clauses (see the revision of **1** above).

(d) Subordinate one of the independent clauses (see the revision of **4** above).

As with comma splices, all four of these ways are usually available for correcting a fused sentence, but in a particular instance, one of them will probably be better than the others. Furthermore, some fused sentences do not readily lend themselves to correction by all four means. For instance, because sentence **1** fuses a question and a statement—**Why am I qualified to speak on this subject** (question) and **I just finished three dreadful years of high school** (statement)—it most readily lends itself to correction by the third method, that of making separate sentences of the two clauses. Sentence **3** does not readily lend itself to correction by the use of a coordinating conjunction. The coordinating conjunctions **or**, **nor**, **for**, **yet**, **so** just do not fit with the sense of the two clauses. Depending on the larger context in which the sentence occurred, joining the two independent clauses with the coordinating conjunctions **and** or **but** might work, but this way of revising the sentence would not be as satisfactory as joining the clauses with a semicolon.

A sentence like **All the apples were picked before the first frost but many of them were unfit to eat**, which lacks a comma before the coordinating conjunction **but**, is not to be regarded as a fused sentence. It lacks the comma in compound sentences called for in **60**, but unlike the examples of fused sentences at the beginning of this section, it has a coordinating conjunction (**but**) to join the two independent clauses.

Reading your prose aloud will usually disclose instances where independent clauses have been run together.

32 Confusing Sentence

Choose words and put them together so that they make sense.

Examples of confusing or puzzling sentences:

1. Much later in the story, the dinner conversation the function of the "small talk" seems to be about the old times.

rewrite:
Much later in the story, the dinner conversation functioned as "small talk" about the old times.

2. The youth, rejected by his parents, by the world, by God, and tragically and ultimately he has rejected himself.

rewrite:
The youth, rejected by his parents, by the world, by God, has tragically and ultimately rejected himself.

3. William Faulkner presents in his short story "Barn Burning" a

human character that is as nonhuman as is feasible to a person's mind.

rewrite:

William Faulkner presents in his short story "Barn Burning" a character that is as unlike a human being as a person could imagine.

32

4. Now in the third stanza, the poet starts her descent. She brings about her conclusion of the boy, which can be paralleled to mankind.

rewrite:

Now in the third stanza, the poet starts her descent. She draws her conclusion about the boy, which is similar to the generalization that could be made about the rest of mankind.

5. Of course, this situation of rundown houses is not always the case, but instead the high rent that the tenants have to pay, which leaves little money for anything else.

rewrite:

Of course, the houses are not invariably rundown, but the high rent that the tenants have to pay leaves little money for anything else.

A confusing or puzzling sentence is one that because of some flaw in the *choice* of words or in the *arrangement* of words reveals no meaning or a scrambled meaning or a vague meaning. Unlike the stylistic flaws discussed in **40**, **41**, and **42**, which produce vague or imprecise or inept sentences, this flaw of diction or arrangement produces what might be called a "non-English" sentence—a sentence that is semantically or grammatically impossible in the English language. For example, a sentence like "The ice cube froze" is a non-English sentence because of the choice of the semantically incompatible words **ice cube** and **froze**. (We can say, "The water froze," but we are uttering nonsense if we say, "The ice cube froze.") A sentence like "Harshly me teacher scolded the yesterday" is a non-English sentence because English grammar does not allow that arrangement of words. To make sense, those words would have to be arranged in an order like "The teacher scolded me harshly yesterday."

Some of the sample sentences are confusing or puzzling mainly because of the choice of words. In sentence **3**, for example, there is some incompatibility between **human character** and **nonhuman**, and the word **feasible** simply does not fit in that context. In sentence **4**, the choice of **conclusion** produced the non-English phrase "her conclusion of the boy." The use of **paralleled** in the final clause of that sentence is an error in idiom, resulting in a non-English clause.

The other sample sentences are examples of confusing or puzzling sentences produced by faulty syntax (arrangement of words). The writers of those sentences started out on a certain track but got derailed, or they switched to another track. Sentence **1**, for instance, starts out well enough—**Much later in the story**, **the dinner conversation** . . . —but then gets derailed. Sentence **2** starts out on one track and then switches to another.

If readers cannot figure out what the writer meant to say, they often cannot analyze what went wrong with the sentence, and they certainly cannot suggest how the bewildering sentence might be fixed up. The best they can do is to point out that the sentence makes no sense and urge the writer to rephrase it.

In the revisions of the sample sentences above, (1) a guess has been made about what the author meant to say, (2) as many of the original words as possible have been retained, and (3) none of the needed stylistic changes have been made. We have merely tried to repair the sentences so that they make sense.

If reading your sentences aloud does not help you detect

confusing or puzzling sentences, you may have to read them aloud to someone else.

33   Proper Form of Verb

Use the proper form of the verb.

Examples of the wrong form of the verb:

1. Before television came along, children **use** to read for hours by the fireplace.

rewrite:
Before television came along, children **used** to read for hours by the fireplace.

2. Whenever I went shopping with my sister, I had the urge to buy everything I **seen**.

rewrite:
Whenever I went shopping with my sister, I had the urge to buy everything I **saw**.

3. In that environment, it seemed that whatever you **would liked** to do was sinful.

rewrite:
In that environment, it seemed that whatever you **would like** to do was sinful.

4. Many parents never ask their children, "**Have** you **drank** your milk yet?"

rewrite:
Many parents never ask their children, "**Have** you **drunk** your milk yet?"

5. Yesterday, when customers **lay** their umbrellas on the counter

while paying their bills, they usually walked off without them.

rewrite:
Yesterday, when customers **laid** their umbrellas on the counter while paying their bills, they usually walked off without them.

33

6. When the incident at Three Mile Island occurred, many people **are frightened**.

rewrite:
When the incident at Three Mile Island occurred, many people **were frightened**.

7. On the top of the hill, there is a sturdy log cabin, which **was** three years old.

rewrite:
On the top of the hill, there is a sturdy log cabin, which **is** three years old.

8. The *Delta Queen* **leaves** Davenport tomorrow. It **will arrive** in St. Louis on Tuesday, and it **stays** there for a day and a half.

rewrite:
The *Delta Queen* **will leave** Davenport tomorrow. It **will arrive** in St. Louis on Tuesday, and it **will stay** there for a day and a half.

Native speakers of English are often not aware of how subtly complicated the English verb system is, especially the system of tenses, which indicate the *time* of an action or a state of being. But foreigners who have to learn English in school are painfully aware of the subtleties of the verb system. English is doubly difficult for those foreigners whose native languages do not have a system of tenses for their verbs. Instead of indicating time by making some change in the *form* of the verb (e.g., **walk—walked**; **sleep—slept**), these languages indicate time by adding some *word* to the sentence—as English sometimes does to indicate future time even when the verb indicates present time (e.g., **She goes tomorrow**).

Native speakers of English, who learn the language in the natural way, as part of the normal process of growing up, usually handle the complicated verb system quite well. Occasionally, however, they use the wrong form of a verb, as did the writers of the sample sentences above. Let us analyze and correct the sample sentences and then review some of the basic conventions governing the formation of the past tense and the past participle of the English verb.

The omission of the -**d** at the end of **use** in a sentence like **1** above is understandable, because in speaking, we are scarcely conscious of pronouncing that final -**d**. But this expression must always be written as **used to**. The verb **drank** in sentence **4** has the past-tense form, but it should have the past-participle form **drunk** so that it will fit with its auxiliary verb **have**. The verb in the *when* clause of sentence **5** clearly needs to be put into the past tense, but the proper form of the past tense of the verb *lay* is **laid**.

Of the three verbs in sentence **2**, one is in the wrong tense; **seen** should be **saw**. This mistake is the reverse of the situation in **4**. The verb in sentence **3** has a -**d** ending that should not be there: **liked** should be **like** (the reverse of **1**). The writer of that sentence may have been influenced to add the -**d** ending to **like** because of the other past-tense signals in the sentence (**seemed**, **would**, and **was**) or because of the sound of **t** in **to** (*like to* = *liket* = *liked*).

Sentences **6**, **7**, and **8** illustrate the error known as **faulty sequence of tenses**—that is, a needless or an unjustifiable shift of tenses in successive clauses or sentences. In sentence **6**, the past tense (**occurred**) in the *when* clause is followed by an incompatible present tense (**are frightened**) in the main clause. Sentence **7** has a present tense (**is**) in the main clause and an unjustifiable past tense (**was**) in the adjective clause. In sentence **8**, there is a sequence of present tense (**leaves**), future tense (**will arrive**), and present tense (**stays**). The context here seems to demand that all three verbs have the future-tense form. But one could also justify putting the three verbs in the present tense (**leave, arrives, stays**).

33

Most of the errors that writers make with verbs involve the lack of agreement in person or number between the subject and predicate or the wrong past-tense form or the wrong past-participle form. Subject-predicate agreement is dealt with in section **22**. This section has dealt mainly with improper past-tense and past-participle forms. The majority of English verbs form their past tense and past participle by adding **-ed** or **-d** to the stem from (e.g., **walk—walked**; **believe—believed**). These verbs are called *regular verbs* or sometimes *weak verbs*.

The so-called *irregular verbs* or *strong verbs* form their past tense and past participle by means of a change in spelling (e.g., **sing—sang—sung**; **hide—hid—hidden**). Most native speakers of English know the principal parts of most of these irregular verbs. When they do not know, or are not sure of, the principal parts, they consult a good dictionary, which regularly supplies the past tense and past participle of all irregular verbs. But for your convenience, the principal parts of some of the most commonly used irregular verbs are presented on the following page. (Incidentally, the *stem form* of the verb is the form that combines with *to* to become the infinitive—**to walk, to go**; the stem form is also the form that the verb has when it is used with the first-person pronouns in the present tense—**I walk, we go**.)

PRINCIPAL PARTS OF SOME IRREGULAR VERBS

stem form	past tense form	past-participle form
begin	began	begun
bite	bit	bitten
blow	blew	blown
break	broke	broken
choose	chose	chosen
do	did	done
drink	drank	drunk
drive	drove	driven
eat	ate	eaten
fall	fell	fallen
fly	flew	flown
forget	forgot	forgotten
give	gave	given
go	went	gone
know	knew	known
lay	laid	laid
lie	lay	lain
pay	paid	paid
ride	rode	ridden
ring	rang	rung
rise	rose	risen
run	ran	run
see	saw	seen
sit	sat	sat
speak	spoke	spoken
swear	swore	sworn
take	took	taken
throw	threw	thrown
wear	wore	worn

33

STYLE

Style is the result of the choices that we make from the available vocabulary and syntactical resources of our language. We may not choose—or should not choose

- **Words and structures that are not part of the language**:

  The defendants have **klinded** the case to the Supreme Court.

  (*no such word in the English language*)

  All gas stations **have being closed** for the duration of the emergency.

  (*no such verb structure in the English language*)

- **Words and structures that make no sense**:

  The mountains lucidly transgressed sentient rocks.

  (*a grammatical but nonsensical sentence*)

- **Words and structures that do not convey a clear, unambiguous meaning**:

  The teacher gave the papers to the students that were chosen by the committee.

  (*was it the **papers** or the **students** that were chosen by the committee?*)

Aside from these unavailable or inadvisable choices, however, the rich vocabulary and the flexible syntax of the English language offer you a number of alternative but synonymous ways of saying something. For instance, you may choose to use an active verb or a passive verb:

> He reported the accident to the police.

> **or**

> The accident was reported by him to the police.

Or you may shift the position of some modifiers:

> He reported the accident to the police when he was ready.

> **or**

> When he was ready, he reported the accident to the police.

Or you may substitute synonymous words and phrases:

> He informed the police about the accident at the intersection.

> **or**

> John notified Sergeant James Murphy about the collision at the corner of Fifth and Main.

A number of other stylistic choices may be open to you:

(a) whether to write a long sentence or to break up the sentence into a series of short sentences.

> (*long sentence*)
>
> In a sense, we did not have history until the invention of the alphabet, because before that invention, the records of national events could be preserved only if there were bards inspired enough to sing about those events and audiences patient enough to listen to a long, metered recitation.

> **or**

> (*a series of short sentences*)
>
> In a sense, we did not have history until the invention of the alphabet. Before that invention, the records of national events were passed on by singing bards. But those bards had to have audiences patient enough to listen to a long, metered recitation.

(b) whether to write a compound sentence or to subordinate one of the clauses.

> (*compound sentence*)
>
> None of the elegies that were delivered at funerals in eighteenth-century village churches have been preserved, but the "short and simple annals of the poor" have been preserved on thousands of gravestones from that era.
>
> **or**
>
> (*subordinate one of the clauses*)
>
> Although none of the elegies that were delivered at funerals in eighteenth-century village churches have been preserved, the "short and simple annals of the poor" have been preserved on thousands of gravestones from that era.

(c) whether to modify a noun with an adjective clause or with a participial phrase or merely with an adjective.

> (*adjective clause*)
>
> The house, which was painted a garish red, did not find a buyer for two months.
>
> **or**
>
> (*participial phrase*)
>
> The house, painted a garish red, did not find a buyer for two months.
>
> **or**
>
> (*adjective*)
>
> The garishly red house did not find a buyer for two months.

(d) whether to use literal language or figurative language.

> (*literal*)
>
> The president walked into a room filled with angry reporters.

or

(*figurative*)

The president walked into a hornet's nest.

(e) whether to use a learned word or an ordinary word (*altercation* or *quarrel*), a specific word or a general word (*sauntered* or *walked*), a formal word or a colloquial word (*children* or *kids*).

(*polysyllabic, formal words*)

Everyone was astonished by her phenomenal equanimity.

or

(*colloquial words*)

Everyone was flabbergasted by her unusual cool.

or

(*ordinary words*)

Everyone was surprised by her composure.

(f) whether to begin a succession of sentences with the same word and the same structure or to vary the diction and the structure.

(*same word, same structure*)

We wanted to preserve our heritage. We wanted to remind our children of our national heroes. We wanted to inspire subsequent generations to emulate our example.

or

(*different words, different structures*)

We wanted to preserve our heritage. Our children, in turn, needed to be reminded of our national heroes. Could we inspire subsequent generations to emulate our example?

The availability of options such as these gives us the opportunity to achieve variety in our style. *By varying the length, the rhythm, and the structure of our sentences, we can avoid monotony, an attention-deadening quality in prose.* The previous sentence is a good example of the variety made possible by the availability of options. All the meanings packed into that sentence could be laid out in a series of short sentences:

> We vary the length of our sentences.
> We vary the rhythm of our sentences.
> We vary the structure of our sentences.
> We can avoid monotony.
> Monotony in prose deadens the attention of readers.

But by a series of transformations that involve **combining** (compounding), **embedding** (subordinating), **shifting** (rearranging), or **deleting** (omitting), we can produce a single neat sentence that emphasizes the main idea and holds the readers' attention. Here is one way that we might have chosen to express all the meanings contained in the five short sentences above:

> If we vary the length, the rhythm, and the structure of our sentences, we can avoid monotony, which deadens readers' attention.

The italicized sentence above represents another way in which all the meanings in the five short sentences could be expressed. By using a different blend of combining, embedding, shifting, and deleting, we could come up with still other ways of expressing all the meanings. The different ways result in different styles.

Choice is the key word in connection with style. Some choices we may not, or should not, make. As was pointed out at the beginning of this section, we may not choose what the grammar of the language does not allow. Furthermore, we cannot choose resources of language that we do not command. We would also be ill-advised to choose words and structures that are inappropriate for the subject matter, the occasion, or the audience.

Aside from those constraints, however, we have hundreds of decisions to make about the choice of vocabulary or syntax while writing. Grammar will determine whether a particular stylistic choice is *correct*—that is, whether a particular locution complies with the conventions of the language. Rhetoric will determine whether a particular stylistic choice is *effective*—that is, whether a particular locution conveys the intended meaning with the clarity, economy, emphasis, and tone appropriate to the subject matter, occasion, audience, and desired effect.

The previous section dealt with what the grammar of the language permits—or, more accurately, with what the conventions of Edited American English permit. This section on style will guide writers in making judicious choices from among the available options. Questions about style are not so much questions about *right* and *wrong* as questions about *good, better, best.*

40   Wrong Word/Faulty Predication

Choose the right word or expression for what you intend to say.

Examples of wrong words or expressions:

1. If you do not **here** from me within three weeks, give me a call.

rewrite:

If you do not **hear** from me within three weeks, give me a call.

2. The shortstop played very **erotically** in the first game of the doubleheader.

rewrite:

The shortstop played very **erratically** in the first game of the doubleheader.

3. The typical surfer has long, **ignominious** hair bleached by the **torpid** sun.

rewrite:

The typical surfer has long, **stringy** hair bleached by the **torrid** sun.

4. A thief and a liar **are vices** that we should avoid.

rewrite:

A thief and a liar **practice vices** that we should avoid.

5. **Abused** children **should not be tolerated** in our society.

rewrite:

The abuse of children **should not be tolerated** in our society.

6. The source of Hemingway's title **is taken** from a sermon by John Donne.

rewrite:

The source of Hemingway's title **is** a sermon by John Donne.

7. The reason she didn't come to class **is because** she was sick.

rewrite:

The reason she didn't come to class **is that** she was sick.

8. The beach **is where** I get my worst sunburn.

rewrite:

The beach **is the place where** I get my worst sunburn.

9. An example of honesty **is when** someone finds a wallet and brings it to the police.

rewrite:

Honesty **is exemplified when** someone finds a wallet and brings it to the police.

40

A word is labeled "wrong" when it does not express the author's intended meaning. The most obvious instance of a "wrong word" is the substitution, usually due to carelessness, of a homonym (a like-sounding word) for the intended word—e.g., **through** for **threw**, **there** for **their**, **sole** for **soul**, **son** for **sun**, **loose** for **lose**. Sentence **1** has one of these homonyms—**here** for **hear**.

Another kind of "wrong word" is called a **malapropism**, after Mrs. Malaprop in Sheridan's play *The Rivals*. Mrs. Malaprop would say things like "as headstrong as an *allegory* on the banks of the Nile," when she should have used the word *alligator*. There is a malapropism in sentence **2**, "Played erratically" is a common phrase, but by using the approximate-sounding word **erotically** in that phrase, the writer has produced a howler.

The occurrence of a "wrong word" is commonly the result of our using a word that is new and somewhat unfamiliar to us. In sentence **3**, the word **ignominious** is wrong for that context. The denotative meaning of the word is "disgraceful," "shameful," but although we can speak of "an ignominious act," the word is "wrong" when applied to **hair**. In the same sentence, if the writer meant to say that the sun was sluggish, **torpid** is the right word; but "torrid sun" comes closer to what the writer probably intended to say.

Wrong words commonly occur as part of the predication of a sentence. This fault is so common that it has acquired its own label—**faulty predication**. A faulty predication occurs when the predicate of a clause (either the verb itself or the whole verb phrase) does not fit semantically or syntactically with the subject of the clause.

Sentences **4**, **5**, and **6** illustrate a semantic mismatch between the subject and the predicate. Thieves and liars cannot be called vices; *thievery* and *lies* are vices. Sentence **5** says that we should not tolerate abused children. Probably what the writer meant to say is that the abuse of children should not be tolerated. In sentence **6**, the predicate **is taken** is incompatible with the subject **source**. It was the title, not the source, that was taken from Donne's sermon.

Sentences **7**, **8**, and **9** illustrate common instances of **faulty predication** involving a syntactical mismatch between the subject and the predicate. The adverb clauses in those sentences cannot serve as complements for the verb **to be**. (No more could a simple adverb serve as the complement of the verb **to be**: "he is swiftly.") One way to correct such faulty predications is to put some kind of nominal structure after the **to be** verb—a noun, a noun phrase, or a noun clause. Avoid this kind of predication:

> The reason is because . . .
> An example is when . . .
> A ghetto is where . . .

41

41 Inexact Word

Choose the precise word for what you want to say.

Examples of imprecise words:

1. I liked the movie *Jewel of the Nile* because it was **interesting**.
rewrite:
> I liked the movie *Jewel of the Nile* because it was continually **suspenseful**.

2. What most impressed me about the poem was the poet's **descriptive** language.
rewrite:
> What most impressed me about the poem was the poet's **vivid**, **sensory** diction.

3. Has-been athletes always have a **sore** look on their faces.
rewrite:
> Has-been athletes always have a **disgruntled** look on their faces.

4. To prevent her from catching a cold, he insisted that she wear the **gigantic** galoshes.

rewrite:

To prevent her from catching cold, he insisted that she wear the **big** galoshes.

5. Honesty is a **thing** that we should value highly.

rewrite:

Honesty is a **virtue** that we should value highly.

6. Jane sold her car, **as** she was planning to take a trip to Europe.

rewrite:

Jane sold her car **because** she was planning to take a trip to Europe.

41

Whereas a "wrong word" misses the target entirely, an "imprecise word" hits all around the bull's-eye and never on dead center. But the governing principle here is that we should strive only for as much precision in diction as the situation demands.

In the spoken medium, diction is often imprecise. But fortunately, in many conversational situations, our diction does not have to be sharply precise in order to communicate adequately. In a conversation, for instance, if someone asked, "How did you like him?" we might respond, "Oh, I thought he was very nice." The word *nice* does not convey a precise meaning, but for the particular situation, it may be precise enough. The word *nice* here, reinforced by our tone of voice, certainly conveys the meaning that we approve of the person, that we are favorably impressed by the person. In speech we do not have the leisure to search for the words that express our meaning exactly. If the woman who asked the question were not satisfied with our general word of approval, *nice*, she could ask us to be more specific about what we meant.

In the written medium, however, we do have the leisure to search for a precise word, and we are not available to the reader who may want or need more specific information than our words supply. Generally, the written medium requires that the words we choose be as exact, as specific, as unequivocal as we can make them. Consulting a thesaurus or, better yet, a dictionary that discriminates the meanings of synonyms will frequently yield the word that conveys our intended meaning precisely.

41

The word **interesting** in sentence 1 is too general to convey a precise meaning. A reader's response to a general word like that would be to ask, "In what way was the movie interesting?" If the writer had said "innovative" or "spellbinding" or "thought-provoking," readers might want some more particulars, but at least they would have a clearer idea of the sense in which the writer considered the movie to be interesting.

The word **descriptive** in sentence 2 is too vague. Expressions like "the poet's simple, concrete words" or "the poet's specific adjectives for indicating colors" would give readers a more exact idea of the kind of descriptive language that impressed the writer of the sentence.

Sore in sentence 3 is ambiguous—that is, it has more than one meaning in its context. The word **sore** could mean either "angry, disgruntled" or "aching, painful." The choice of a more exact word here will clarify the writer's meaning.

Gigantic in sentence 4 above is exaggerated. Unless the word were deliberately chosen to create a special effect of humor or irony, the writer should use a word more proportionate to the circumstances, such as *big* or *heavy* or *ungainly*.

In the oral medium, we can get by with a catchall word like **thing**, as in sentence 5, but writing allows us the leisure to search for a word that will serve as a more accurate predicate complement for *honesty*. We can use words like *policy*, *virtue*, *habit*, *disposition*—whichever fits best with what we want to say about honesty here.

The subordinating conjunction **as** carries a variety of meanings, and it is not always possible to tell from the context which of its several meanings it carries in a particular sentence. In sentence **6**, we cannot tell whether **as** is being used in its sense of "because" or "since" or "when" or "while." We should use the conjunction that exactly expresses our intended meaning: **because** she was planning; **when** she was planning; **while** she was planning. We should reserve the conjunction **as** for those contexts in which there is no possibility of ambiguity, as in sentences like "In that kind of situation, he acts exactly **as** he should" and "Do **as** I say."

42 Inappropriate Word

Choose words that are appropriate to the context.

Examples of inappropriate words:

1. He didn't want to **exacerbate** his mother's **sangfroid**, so he **indited** an **epistolary message** to inform her of his unavoidable **retardation**.

rewrite:

He didn't want to **upset** his mother, so he **wrote** her a **note** to inform her that **he would be late**.

2. Whenever I visit a new city, I browse through a secondhand bookstore and eventually **cheapen** a book.

rewrite:

Whenever I visit a new city, I browse through a secondhand bookstore and eventually **bid** for a book.

3. The conclusion that I have come to is that **kids** should not have to suffer for the sins of their fathers.

rewrite:

The conclusion that I have come to is that **children** should not have to suffer for the sins of their fathers.

4. Merchants in areas where the freeway would be built have persistently opposed the project, claiming that it would **freak out** the residents.

rewrite:

Merchants in areas where the freeway would be built have persistently opposed the project, claiming that it would **disconcert** the residents.

42

A word is inappropriate if it does not fit, if it is out of tune with, the subject matter, the occasion, the audience, or the personality of the writer. It is a word that is conspicuously "out of place" with its environment.

No word in isolation can be labeled inappropriate; it must first be seen in the company of other words. Although we would feel safer in making a judgment if we had a larger context, the boldfaced words in the sample sentences above seem to be inappropriate.

Sentence **1** exhibits the kind of language used by (usually beginning) writers who are passing through a phase in which they seem unable to say even a simple thing in a simple way. New writers consciously striving to enlarge their vocabulary often produce sentences like this one. Instead of using a thesaurus to find an accurate or precise word, they use it to find an unusual or polysyllabic word that they think will make their prose sound "literary" or learned or both. The label sometimes applied to such pretentious, ornate diction is "purple prose." Fortunately, most of those who are ambitious enough to want to expand their working vocabulary eventually develop enough sophistication to be able to judge when the language they choose is appropriate and when it is not.

Sentence **2** illustrates another kind of inappropriateness. The word **cheapen** was once a perfectly appropriate word as used in this context. During the Elizabethan period in England, it was a common verb meaning "to bid for," "to bargain for." If you look up the word in a modern dictionary, you will discover that **cheapen** in this sense is labeled archaic. The label means that the word in that sense can no longer be used in a modern context.

The more common fault of inappropriateness, however, is diction that is too colloquial or too slangy for its context. This fault is illustrated in sentences **3** and **4**. Although there are contexts in which the colloquial word **kids** would be more appropriate than the word *children*, sentence **3** seems not to be one of those contexts. There are contexts where slang and even the jargon of particular social groups would be perfectly appropriate, but the slang in sentence **4** seems to be out of tune with the subject matter and with almost all of the other words in the sentence.

Since dictionaries, thesauruses, and handbooks will not be of much help in telling you that a word is inappropriate, you will have to rely on the criteria of subject matter, occasion, audience, desired effect, and personality of the author. Another way of putting this precept is to say that your "voice" must remain in harmony with the overall tone that you have established in a particular piece of writing.

43 Unidiomatic Expression

Use the proper idiom.

Examples of lapse of idiom:

1. Although I **agree to** a few of Socrates's principles, I must **disagree to** many of them.

rewrite:

Although I **agree with** a few of Socrates's principles, I must **disagree with** many of them.

2. Formerly **devoted on** a theatrical career, she developed a strong **passion in** gourmet cooking.

rewrite:

Formerly **devoted to** a theatrical career, she developed a strong **passion for** gourmet cooking.

3. Conformity has been a common tendency throughout **the** American history.

rewrite:

Conformity has been a common tendency throughout American history.

4. Nobody seems **immune from** pressures.

rewrite:

Nobody seems **immune to** pressures.

5. It's these special characters and their motives that I **intend on concentrating** in this paper.

rewrite:

It's these special characters and their motives that I **intend to concentrate on** in this paper.

6. Abner had no **interest** or **respect for** the boy.

rewrite:

Abner had no **interest in** or **respect for** the boy.

To label a locution unidiomatic is to indicate that native speakers of the language do not say it that way—in any dialect of the language. Unidiomatic expressions are one of the most common weaknesses to be found in the prose of unpracticed writers. Why lapses of idiom occur so frequently is a good question to ask, because writers presumably do not hear other native speakers use the curious expressions that they write down on paper. One explanation for the frequency of idiomatic lapses is that unpracticed writers use words and structures that they seldom or never use in speech; and because they have not paid close enough attention to the way native speakers say something, they make a guess—usually a wrong guess—at how the expression should be phrased.

No word by itself is ever unidiomatic. Only combinations of words can be unidiomatic. The most common kind of idiomatic lapse is the one that occurs with a preposition. Three of the first four sample sentences above involve idiomatic lapses in the use of prepositions.

43

A number of prepositions fit idiomatically with the verbs **agree** and **disagree**, but the preposition that fits idiomatically with the sense of **agree** and **disagree** in sentence **1** is **with**. There will be other contexts when the correct preposition to use with **agree** will be **to** ("They agreed to the conditions we laid down") or **on** ("They can't agree on the wording of the proposal").

There are two unidiomatic prepositions in sentence **2**. Native speakers don't say "devoted **on**" or "a passion **in**"; they say "devoted **to**" and "a passion **for**." In a sentence like **4**, above, native speakers don't say "immune **from**"; they say "immune **to**."

No native speaker of English would use the article **the** in the phrase **throughout the American history** (see sentence **3**). However, whereas a British speaker would say, "He was in hospital" (without **the**), an American speaker would use **the**: "He was in the hospital." Some speakers for whom English is a second language have trouble with the English article because their language does not use a part of speech like it.

Sentence **5** above is clearly an instance of a writer's using a structure that he or she has never attempted before and failing to recall how native speakers phrase it. The structure should be phrased in this way: "intend **to concentrate on**."

Unidiomatic expressions often appear in compounded phrases, as in sentence **6**. The preposition **for** fits with **respect** ("respect **for** the boy"), but it does not fit with **interest** (not "interest **for** the boy" but "interest **in** the boy"). In such cases, the idiomatic preposition must be inserted for both members of the compound.

What prevents a handbook from setting reliable guidelines for proper idiom is the fact that logic plays little or no part in establishing the idioms of a language. If logic were involved in establishing idioms, we would say, "He looked *down* the word in the dictionary" instead of what we do say, "He looked *up* the word in the dictionary." Editors or teachers can call your attention to an unidiomatic expression and can insert the correct idiom, but they cannot give you rules that will prevent other lapses of idiom. You simply have to learn proper idioms by reading and listening attentively.

44

44   Trite Expression

Avoid trite expressions.

Examples of trite expressions:

1. I returned from the picnic **tired but happy**, and that night I **slept like a log**.

rewrite:

I returned from the picnic tired but content, and that night I slept soundly.

2. My primary objective in coming to college was to get a **well-rounded education**.

rewrite:

My primary objective in coming to college was to get a balanced education.

3. The construction of two new hotels was a **giant step forward** for the community.

rewrite:
The construction of two new hotels represented significant progress for the community.

4. In the last few years, the popularity of ice hockey has grown **by leaps and bounds**.

rewrite:
In the last few years, the popularity of ice hockey has grown immensely.

5. Convinced now that drugs are a temptation for young people, the community must **nip the problem in the bud** before it **runs rampant**.

rewrite:
Convinced now that drugs are a temptation for young people, the community must solve the problem before it gets out of control.

There is nothing grammatically or idiomatically wrong with a trite expression. A trite expression is *stylistically* objectionable—mainly because it is a *tired* expression. Whether an expression is "tired" is, of course, a relative matter. What is lackluster for some readers may be bright-penny new for others. But it would be surprising if the expressions in the examples above were not jaded for most readers.

Trite expressions are certain combinations of words or certain figures of speech that have been used so often that they have lost their freshness and even their meaning for most readers. Rhetorically, the price that you pay for using trite language is the alienation of your readers. Readers stop paying attention. You may have something new and important to say, but if your message is delivered in threadbare language, you will lose or fail to capture the attention of your readers.

Figures of speech are especially prone to staleness. Metaphors like "nip in the bud," "slept like a log," "giant step" were once fresh and cogent; they are now wilted from overuse. Trite combinations of words like "tired but happy," "by leaps and bounds," "runs rampant" produce glazed-eyed readers. Ironically, one of the ways in which to revise sentences that have trite language is to use the most familiar, ordinary language. Sentence **1**, for example, would be improved if **but content** were substituted for **but happy** and if a simple adverb, like **soundly**, were substituted for the simile **like a log**. Notice how familiar, literal words are substituted for the stale metaphors in sentences **3**, **4**, and **5**.

44

Sometimes, making a daring alteration in a tired expression can rejuvenate the sentence. Look at what happens to the yawn-producing **well-rounded education** in this revision of sentence **2**:

> My primary objective in coming to college was to get a well-squared education.

If you make an effort to invent your own figures of speech, you may produce awkward, strained figures, but at least they will be fresh. Instead of borrowing the hackneyed metaphor **nip the problem in the bud**, make up your own metaphor:

> Convinced now that drugs are a temptation for young people, the community should excise the tumor before it becomes a raging cancer.

It takes a great deal of sophistication about language even to recognize trite expressions, and those who don't read very much can hardly be expected to detect tired language because almost all the expressions that they encounter are relatively new to them. They may have to rely on others to point out the trite language in their prose.

Be wary of weary words.

45 Awkward Sentence

Rephrase awkwardly constructed sentences.

Examples of awkward sentences:

1. You could get a dose of the best exercise a person could undertake, walking. I believe a person should walk at a leisurely pace, with no set goal on distance.

rewrite:
> The best exercise for people is walking at a leisurely pace as far as they feel like going.

2. The football player has had many broken noses, with which he ends up looking like a prizefighter.

rewrite:
> The football player has broken his nose so often that he looks like a prizefighter.

3. I and probably everybody else who started drinking beer in their sophomore year of high school thought the only thing to do was get drunk and go to school activities where we could meet and have a good time.

rewrite:
> Like everybody else who started drinking beer as a high school sophomore, I thought that being drunk while going to school activities would be the best way to ensure a good time.

The fault dealt with in **32**, in the Grammar section, concerns sentences that are so badly put together that they reveal no meaning or only a vague meaning. Awkward sentences, which are dealt with in this section, are sentences so ineptly put together that they are difficult—but not impossible—for readers to understand. They are sentences that are grammatically passable but stylistically weak.

Those who write awkwardly constructed sentences are usually not aware that they are doing so; they have to be told that their sentences are awkward. If they adopt the practice of reading their sentences aloud, they will often detect clumsy, odd-sounding combinations of words. Thus alerted, they can then examine their sentences for the presence of any of the usual causes of awkwardness:

(a) Excessive number of words (see sentence **3**)

(b) Words and phrases out of their normal order (note the position of **walking** in sentence **1**)

(c) Successions of prepositional phrases ("the president of the largest chapter of the national fraternity of students of dentistry")

(d) Pretentious circumlocutions ("the penultimate month of the year" for "November")

(e) Split constructions ("I, chastened by my past experiences, resolved to never consciously and maliciously circulate, even if true, damaging reports about my friends")

(f) Successions of rhyming words ("She tries wisely to revise the evidence supplied by her eyes")

The sample sentences at the beginning of this section are awkward for a variety of reasons. Pruning some of the deadwood, rearranging some of the parts, using simpler, more idiomatic phrases, we can improve the articulation of those clumsy sentences.

Construct your sentences so smoothly that your readers won't have to stumble through them.

46 Wordy Sentence

Cut out unnecessary words.

Examples of wordy sentences:

1. He was justified in trying to straighten out his mother on her backward ideas about her attitude toward blacks.

rewrite:

> He was justified in trying to straighten out his mother's attitude toward blacks. (from 19 to 13 words)

2. In this modern world of today, we must get an education that will prepare us for a job in our vocation in life.

rewrite:

> In the modern world, we must get an education that will prepare us for a job. (from 23 to 16 words)

3. In the "Garden of Love," the poem relates the sad experience of a child being born into a cruel world.

rewrite:

> "The Garden of Love" relates the sad experience of a child born into a cruel world. (from 20 to 16 words)

4. The meaning, at least in my own eyes, that he is trying to convey in the poem "Arms and the Boy" is of the evilness of war in that it forces innocent people to take up the instrument of death and destruction and then tries to teach them to love to use them to kill other human beings.

rewrite:

> As I see it, the poet's thesis in "Arms and the Boy" is that war is evil, because it not only forces people to take up arms but makes them use these weapons to kill other human beings. (from 58 to 38 words)

5. These rivers do not contain fish, due to the fact that the flow of water is too rapid.

rewrite:

> These rivers do not contain fish because the water flows too rapidly. (from 18 to 12 words)

A "wordy sentence" is one in which a writer has used more words than are needed to say what has to be said. The superfluous words simply clutter up a sentence and impede its movement. Speakers are especially prone to verbosity because words come so easily to their tongues. But writers

too are prone to verbosity once they acquire a certain facil-
ity with words. Facile writers have to make a conscious
effort to control their expenditure of words. Writers would
soon learn to cultivate restraint if they were charged for
every word used, as they are when they send a telegram.
They should not, of course, strive for a "telegraphic" or a
"headline" style, but they should learn to value words so
much that they spend words sparingly.

Each of the revised sentences uses fewer words than the
original. The reduction ranges from four words to twenty
words. If the writers were being charged a quarter a word,
they could probably find other superfluous words to
prune. The writer of the fourth sentence, for instance,
would lop off **As I see it** and would condense **to kill other
human beings** to **to kill others**.

One should not become obsessed with saving words, but
one should seize every opportunity, in the revising stage, to
clear out obvious deadwood. As Alexander Pope said,

> Words are like leaves, and where they most abound,
> Much fruit of sense beneath is rarely found.

47 Repetition

Avoid careless or needless repetition of words and ideas.

Examples of careless or needless repetition:

1. Mrs. Bucks, a **fellow colleague**, offered to intercede with the
dean.

rewrite:

Mrs. Bucks, a **colleague**, offered to intercede with the dean.

2. He does not rely on the **surrounding environment** as much as his sister does.

rewrite:

He does not rely on the **environment** as much as his sister does.

3. The objective point of view accentuates the emotional intensity of the love affair and the **impending** failure that will **eventually happen**.

rewrite:

The objective point of view accentuates the emotional intensity of the love affair and its **impending failure**.

47

4. In Larry's mind, he **thinks**, "I have never met anyone so absorbed in himself."

rewrite:

Larry thinks, "I have never met anyone so absorbed in himself."

5. There are some striking similarities between Segal and Hemingway, for **both** have studied life and love and found them **both** to be failures.

rewrite:

There are some striking similarities between Segal and Hemingway, for **both** found life and love to be failures.

6. After **setting** up camp, we **set** off to watch the sun **set**.

rewrite:

After **preparing** camp, we **took off** to watch the sun **set**.

7. Please remain in your seats until the aircraft comes to a **complete stop** at the gate.

rewrite:

Please remain in your seats until the aircraft comes to a **stop** at the gate.

A "careless or needless repetition" refers either to the recurrence of a word in the same sentence or in adjoining sentences or to the use of synonymous words that produces what is called a **redundancy** or a **tautology**.

The emphasis in this caution about repetition should be put on the words *careless* and *needless*, for there are cases where repetition serves a purpose. Item **51** in the next section, for instance, shows that the repetition of key words can be an effective means of achieving coherence in a paragraph. Sometimes it is better to repeat a word, even in the same sentence, than to run the risk of ambiguity or misunderstanding. In the first sentence of this paragraph, for example, the word **repetition** has been repeated because the use of the pronoun *it* in place of **repetition** would be ambiguous (we would wonder whether that pronoun **it** referred to **emphasis** or **repetition**).

48

The boldfaced words in the first four sentences and in sentence **7** are instances of redundancy or tautology (needless repetition of the same idea in different words). **Fellow** and **colleague**, **surrounding** and **environment**, **impending** and **eventually happen**, **complete** and **stop** are examples of needless repetition. In sentence **4**, the phrase **In Larry's mind** is superfluous (where else does one **think** but in the mind?). The repetition of the pronoun **both** in sentence **5** is especially careless because the repeated pronouns have different antecedents, thus producing confusion (the first one refers to **Segal** and **Hemingway**, the second to **life** and **love**). In sentence **6**, we have an instance of the same basic verb form (**set**) repeated in three different senses.

48   Figurative Language

Avoid mixed metaphors.

Examples of mixed metaphors:

1. Sarty finally comes to the point where his inner turmoil reaches its **zenith** and **stagnates in a pool** of lethargy.

rewrite:
> Sarty finally comes to the point where his inner turmoil reaches its **zenith** and then **plummets into a pool** of lethargy.

2. In "The Dead," James Joyce uses small talk as an effective **weapon** to **illustrate** his thesis.

rewrite:
> In "The Dead," James Joyce uses small talk as a **mirror** to **reflect** his thesis.

3. She tried to **scale the wall** of indifference but found that she couldn't **burrow** through it.

rewrite:
> She tried to **scale the wall** of indifference but found that she couldn't **surmount** it.

4. The experience struck a **spark** that **massaged** the poet's imagination.

rewrite:
> The experience struck a **spark** that **ignited** the poet's imagination.

5. When we tried to get the mayor's campaign **off the ground**, we found that it **sank in a sea** of apathy.

rewrite:
> When we tried to get the mayor's campaign **off the ground**, we found that it didn't **get up enough speed to become airborne**.

A mixed metaphor is the result of a writer's failure to keep a consistent image in mind. All metaphors are based on the perceived likenesses between things that exist in different orders of being—as for instance between a *man* and a *greyhound* ("The lean shortstop is a greyhound when he runs the bases"), *fame* and a *spur* ("Fame is the spur to ambition"), *mail* and an *avalanche* ("The mail buried the staff under an avalanche of complaints"). Whenever any detail is incompatible with one or other of the terms of the analogy, the metaphor is said to be mixed.

Zenith, in sentence **1**, connotes something rising to its highest point, and therefore that image of ascending motion is incompatible with the detail of **stagnation**. Likewise, a **weapon** is not used to **illustrate** something. If one were climbing (**scaling**) a wall, one could not dig (**burrow**) through it at the same time. A **spark** could start a fire, but it couldn't **massage** anything. The basic metaphor in the first half of the fifth sentence is that of an airplane taking off, but in the second half of the sentence, the metaphor shifts to that of a ship sinking.

Forming and maintaining a clear picture of the notion you are attempting to express figuratively will ensure a consistent metaphor.

49

49   Passive Verb

Consider whether an active verb would be preferable to a passive verb.

Examples of questionable use of the passive voice:

1. Money **was borrowed** by the couple so that they could pay off all their bills.

rewrite:

The couple **borrowed** money so that they could pay off all their bills.

2. His love for her **is shown** by his accepting her story and by his remaining at her side when she is in trouble.

rewrite:

He **shows** his love for her by accepting her story and by remaining at her side when she is in trouble.

3. From these recurrent images of hard, resistant metals, it **can be inferred** by us that she was a mechanical, heartless person.

rewrite:

> From these recurrent images of hard, resistant metals, we **can infer** that she was a mechanical, heartless person.

4. Talking incessantly, he **was overwhelmed** by the teacher.

rewrite:

> Talking incessantly, the teacher **overwhelmed** him.

49

If the use of a passive verb is questionable, it is questionable stylistically, not grammatically. To question the use of a passive verb is to ask the writer to consider whether the sentence would not be more emphatic or more economical or less awkward or somehow "neater" if an active verb were used. Challenged to consider the options available in a particular case, the writer is the final judge of the best choice in that case.

Writers sometimes decide to use the passive verb because they want to give special emphasis to some word in the sentence. In sentence 1, the word **money** gets special emphasis because it occupies the initial position. If the active verb were used, the word **couple** would get the special emphasis. It would be more difficult to cite emphasis as the justification for the choice of passive verbs in sentences 2 and 3. Writers can also justify the use of a passive verb when they do not know the agent of an action or prefer not to reveal the agent or consider it unnecessary to indicate the agent, as in the sentence "The story was reported to all the newspapers."

Dangling verbals often result from the use of a passive verb in the main clause of the sentence (see 25 on dangling verbals.) The context of sentence 4 suggests that the lead-off participial phrase (**talking incessantly**) may be dangling—that is, that it was not the man or boy (**he**) but **the teacher** who was talking incessantly. If that is so, the writer may not choose the passive verb for the main clause but must use the active verb.

PARAGRAPHING

One way to regard paragraphing is to view it as a system of punctuating stages of thought presented in units larger than the word and the sentence. Paragraphing is a means of alerting readers to a shift of focus in the development of the main idea of the whole discourse. It marks off for the reader's convenience the individually distinct but related parts of the whole discourse. How paragraphing facilitates reading would be made dramatically evident if a whole discourse were written or printed—as ancient manuscripts once were—in a single, unbroken block.

Like punctuation and mechanics, paragraphing is a feature only of the written language. Some linguists claim that speakers of connected discourse signal their "paragraphs" by pauses and by shifts in the tone of their voice. (The next time you hear a speech being delivered from a written text, see if you can detect when the speaker shifts to another paragraph of his or her text.) But speakers are not conscious—especially in extemporaneous stretches of talk—of paragraphing the stream of sound as writers must be when they are writing their manuscripts.

The typographical device most commonly used to mark off paragraphs is *indentation*. The first line of each new paragraph starts several spaces (usually five spaces on the typewriter) from the left-hand margin. Another convention for marking paragraphs is the block system: beginning the first line at the left-hand margin but leaving double or triple spacing between paragraphs. One of the forms of writing that regularly uses the block system is the single-spaced, typewritten business letter.

In this section, only three aspects of the paragraph are treated: unity, coherence, and adequate development. The traditional means of developing the central idea of a paragraph are mentioned in the section on adequate development, but they are not discussed at length. The means of developing paragraphs are fundamentally a concern of invention, which is the province of a rhetoric text rather than of a handbook. However, if you take care of unity, coherence, and adequate development, you will be attending to the three most persistent and common problems that beset the composition of written paragraphs.

50

50 Unity

Preserve the unity of the paragraph.

The principle governing paragraph unity is that a paragraph should develop a single topic or thesis, which is often—but not always—announced in a topic sentence. Every sentence in the paragraph should contribute in some way to the development of that single idea. When writers introduce other ideas into the paragraph, they violate the unity of the paragraph and disorient their readers.

Example of a paragraph lacking unity:

1. The eminence of Samuel Johnson inclines modern scholars to study his thoughts and opinions. His multifarious knowledge intrigued his contemporaries. Although he manifested his in-

terest in the drama by editing Shakespeare, he did not enjoy the theater. He was envious too of his former pupil David Garrick, the greatest actor of the eighteenth century.

The first sentence of paragraph **1**, which has the air of being a "topic sentence," mentions that modern scholars have turned their attention to a study of Samuel Johnson. Instead of the second sentence going on to develop that idea, it mentions what Dr. Johnson meant to his contemporaries. The third sentence talks about his attitude toward drama and the theater. The fourth sentence mentions his envy of his former pupil David Garrick. What we have in this paragraph is four topics. A whole paragraph or paper could be devoted to the development of each of these four topics, but here they are packed into a single paragraph.

50

The following presents one of the ways in which the paragraph might be revised to give it unity:

> The eminence of Samuel Johnson inclines modern scholars to study his thoughts and opinions. A number of recent books and articles have dealt with his viewpoints on a variety of his interests. One of those interests was the drama. Curiously, however, although he manifested this interest by writing his own play for the stage and by editing all the plays of Shakespeare, he did not enjoy the theater. Some modern scholars have speculated that he did not enjoy the theater because of his poor eyesight and impaired hearing. Others have speculated that he disliked the theater because he was jealous of his former pupil David Garrick, who very early in his career acquired the reputation of being the greatest actor of his day.

Another example of a paragraph lacking unity:

2. "The Cradle Song" from the *Songs of Innocence* has internal rhyme. In this poem, the child is quiet and happy. It has a heavenly image, and throughout the poem, the mother sheds tears of joy. It has a persona—that is, one who speaks for the

poet—who is naive and innocent. The poem "Infant Sorrow" contrasts with "The Cradle Song," and this contrast is very distinct. One can see a screaming and devilish child. The piping is a harsh sound, and the child, who's against restrictions, is looking back and realizing that there is no paradise on earth.

Paragraph **2** has a certain unity: each sentence is saying something about a poem by William Blake. Even though this paragraph discusses two different poems by Blake, we can detect some unity in the paragraph if we view it as developing a contrast between two poems by the same author. And, indeed, midway through the paragraph, the writer explicitly announces that the two poems contrast with one another. But even if we were generous enough to concede that much unity to the paragraph, it would be difficult for us to perceive a unifying theme among the many disparate things said about the two poems.

Here is a revision of that paragraph to give it unity:

William Blake's "The Cradle Song" contrasts distinctly with his poem "Infant Sorrow." Whereas the child in "The Cradle Song" is quiet and happy, the child in "Infant Sorrow" is strident and devilish. Both poems have a persona—that is, one who speaks for the poet—but the persona in "The Cradle Song" is naive and innocent, whereas the persona in the other poem is worldly-wise and guilt-ridden. The rhythms and rhymes in the first poem are smooth and pleasant, but the rhythms and rhymes of the second poem are harsh and discordant. One poem presents an overall mood of contentment; the other presents a mood of disillusionment.

Here is a third example of a disunified paragraph:

3. Dr. Rockwell let his feelings be known on only one subject: the administration. He felt that the administrative system was outdated. Abolishing grades, giving the student a voice in administration, and revamping the curriculum were three steps he felt should be taken to improve the system. Dr. Rockwell

50

taught in this manner. In class, a mysterious aura surrounded him. He was "hip" to what was going on, but he preferred to hear the members of the class rather than himself. He was quiet and somewhat shy. His eyes caught everything that went on in class. His eyes generated a feeling of understanding.

Paragraph 3 also has a certain unity: each sentence in the paragraph is talking about the teacher Dr. Rockwell. And there is a tight unity in the first three sentences: each of these sentences talks about Dr. Rockwell's attitude toward the administration. But with the fourth sentence of the paragraph, the writer introduces another and unrelated topic: a description of how Dr. Rockwell conducted himself in the classroom. If the writer had broken up this stretch of prose into two paragraphs and had reorganized some of the sentences, each of the two paragraphs would have had its own unity:

> Dr. Rockwell let his feelings be known on only one subject: the administration. His estimate of the administrative system of the school was largely negative. He felt, for instance, that the administrative system was outdated. Abolishing grades, giving students a voice in administration, and revamping the curriculum were three steps he felt should be taken to improve the system.
>
> Dr. Rockwell's demeanor in the classroom was remarkable. Although there was a mysterious aura about him, he was always "hip" to what was going on. His eyes caught everything that went on in class, but they generated a feeling of understanding. Even though he was a very learned scholar, this quiet, somewhat shy man preferred to listen to the members of the class rather than himself.

A paragraph will have unity, will have "oneness," if every sentence in it has an obvious bearing on the development of a single topic. When writers sense that they have shifted to the discussion of another topic, they should begin a new paragraph.

50

51 Coherence

Compose the paragraph so that it reads coherently.

Coherence is that quality which makes it easy for a reader to follow a writer's train of thought from sentence to sentence and from paragraph to paragraph. Coherence facilitates reading because it ensures that the reader will be able to detect the relationship of the parts of a discourse. It also reflects the clear thinking of the writer because it results from the writer's arrangement of ideas in some kind of perceptible order and from the use of those verbal devices that help to stitch thoughts together. In short, as the Latin roots of the word suggest (*co*, "together," + *haerēre*, "to stick"), coherence helps the parts of a discourse "stick together."

Here are some ways in which to achieve coherence in a paragraph (not all of these devices, of course, have to be used in every paragraph):

(a) Repeat key words from sentence to sentence or use recognizable synonyms for key words.

(b) Use pronouns for key nouns. (Because a pronoun gets its meaning from the noun to which it refers, it is by its very nature one of those verbal devices that help to stitch sentences together.)

(c) Use demonstrative adjectives, "pointing words" (**this** statement, **that** plan, **these** developments, **those** disasters).

(d) Use conjunctive adverbs, "thought-connecting words" (**however, moreover, also, nevertheless, therefore, thus, subsequently, indeed, then, accordingly**).

(e) Arrange the sequence of sentences in some kind of perceivable order (for instance, a **time order**, as in a narrative of what happened or in an explanation of how to do something; a **space order**, as in the description of a physical object or a scene; a **logical order**, such as cause to effect, effect to cause, general to particular, particular to general, whole to part, familiar to unfamiliar).

Here is an example of an incoherent paragraph:

> After the program has been written, each line is punched onto a card. The deck of cards is known as the "program source deck." The next step is to load the program compiler into the computer. The compiler is a program written in machine language for a particular computer, which reads the source deck and performs a translation of the program language into machine language. The machine language, in the form of instructions, is punched onto cards. This machine-language deck of cards is known as the "object deck." After the object deck has been punched, the programmer is then able to execute his program. The program is run by loading the object deck into the computer. The run of the program marks the end of the second step.

51

This paragraph attempts to describe computer programming, a process that most readers would find difficult to follow because it is unfamiliar and complicated. But the process will be doubly difficult for readers if it is not described coherently. What makes this description of computer programming especially difficult to follow is that the writer is doing two things at once in the paragraph: (1) designating the chronological sequence of steps in the process, and (2) defining the technical terms used in the description of the process. It would have been better if the writer had devoted one paragraph to defining such terms as **program source deck**, **compiler**, **object deck**. Then the writer could have devoted another paragraph exclusively to the description of the process of "running a program"— first you do this, then you do that, after that you do this, etc. As the paragraph now stands, readers get lost because they are kept bouncing back and forth between definition of the terms and description of the process.

Here is a revision of that paragraph:

> Before you can understand the process of "running a program," you need some definitions of technical terms. After the program discussed in the previous paragraph has been written, each line of that program is punched onto an IBM card. The collection of these cards is known as the "program source deck." Another set of cards is known as the "compiler." The compiler "reads" the source deck and translates it into machine language, which is then punched onto IBM cards. The machine-language deck of cards that results from the operation of the compiler is known as the "object deck."
>
> The first step in the process is to put the program source deck into the computer. Then in order to translate the program language of the source deck into machine language, the compiler set must be inserted. Following that step, the object deck, with its instructions written out in machine language, is put into the computer. Now the program is ready to be "run" through the computer.

Here are two more examples of incoherent paragraphs:

1. The first stanza of "The Echoing Green" does not correspond with any other poem by Blake. The glory of nature's beauty is presented in vivid details. Emotional intensity is the overall effect of the poem. Blake resents the mechanization which has been brought about by the Industrial Revolution. The rhythm of the verses contributes to the meditative mood.

2. The preceding account illustrates all the frustrations that a beginning golfer experiences. The dominant philosophy is that the golfer who looks the best plays the best. He complicates the game by insisting on perfection the first time he sets foot on the course. More time and money are spent on clothes and equipment than on the most important aspect, skill. Win-

ning is the only goal. Where is the idea of recreation? Try playing without a caddy sometime, and see how much exercise you get.

It is difficult to suggest ways of revising paragraphs 1 and 2 because they are so incoherent that it is almost impossible to discover what the principal points were that the writers wanted to put across in them. If we could confer with the writers and ask them what the main idea of their paragraphs was supposed to be, we could then advise them about which of the sentences contributed to the development of that idea (and which sentences had to be dropped because they threatened the unity of the paragraph), about the order of the sentences in the given paragraph, and about the verbal devices that would help to knit the sequence of sentences together.

Each of the following revisions constitutes one of a number of ways in which the two paragraphs might be written to give them some coherence:

1. It is interesting to note how William Blake achieves the emotional intensity that he does in "The Echoing Green." He achieves that intensity partly by presenting the glory of nature in vivid details that contrast with the dull, gray mechanization of the urban scene that has been produced by the Industrial Revolution. The slow rhythm of the verses also contributes to the emotional intensity by creating a meditative mood. The extraordinary collection of images in the first stanza of the poem also serves to exert a strong emotional effect on the reader.

2. The beginning golfer is often frustrated by the false sense of values that he has been sold. For one thing, he spends more time and money on buying clothes and equipment than on acquiring the most important aspect, skill. Apparently, he has bought the philosophy that the golfer who looks the best plays the best. Moreover, because he has bought the philosophy that

winning is the only goal, he has lost sight of the goal of recreation. He insists on perfection the first time he sets foot on the course instead of being satisfied with the fun and exercise he gets from playing a round of eighteen holes.

Coherence is a difficult writing skill to master, but until you acquire at least a measure of that skill, you will continue to be frustrated in your efforts to communicate with others on paper. You must learn how to compose paragraphs so that the sequence of thoughts flows smoothly, easily, and logically from sentence to sentence. You must provide those bridges or links that will allow the reader to pass from sentence to sentence without being puzzled about the relationship of what is said in one sentence to what is said in the next sentence.

52 Development

Paragraphs should be adequately developed.

Generally, one- and two-sentence paragraphs are not justifiable, except for purposes of emphasis, transition, or dialogue.

Note that this last sentence is also a paragraph, justifiable as such on the grounds that the writer wanted to give special emphasis to a principle by setting it aside in a paragraph by itself. Separate paragraphing for emphasis is a graphic device comparable to underlining a word or a phrase in a sentence for emphasis. Set aside in a paragraph by itself, an important idea achieves a prominence that would be missed if the idea were merged with other ideas in the same paragraph.

A one- or two-sentence paragraph can also be used to mark or signal a transition from one major division of a discourse to the next major division. These transitional paragraphs facilitate reading because they orient readers, reminding them of what has been discussed and alerting them to what is going to be discussed. Such paragraphs are like signposts marking the major stages of a journey. Note how the following two-sentence transitional paragraph looks backward to what has been discussed and forward to what will be discussed:

> After presenting his introduction to *Songs of Experience,* William Blake apparently feels that his readers have been sufficiently warned about their earthly predicament. Let us see now how he uses the poems in *Songs of Experience* to illustrate what the people might do to solve their problems.

52

One of the conventions of printing is that in representing dialogue in a story, we should begin a new paragraph every time the speaker changes. A paragraph of dialogue can be one sentence long or ten sentences long (any number of sentences, in fact). A paragraph of dialogue may also consist of only a phrase or a single word. Note the paragraphing of the following stretch of dialogue:

> "Look at that cloudless blue sky," Melvin said. "There doesn't seem to be any bottom to that blue. It's beautiful, isn't it?"
>
> "Yup," Hank muttered.
>
> "Remember yesterday?"
>
> "Yup."
>
> "I thought it would never stop raining."
>
> "Me too."

Once an exchange like that gets going, the author can dispense with the identifying tags, because each separate paragraph will mark the shift in speaker.

But except for the purposes of emphasis, transition, or dialogue, a one- or a two-sentence paragraph can rarely be justified. One sentence is hardly enough to qualify as both the topic sentence and the development of the idea posed by that topic. Many times even three- and four-sentence paragraphs are not adequately developed. You will frequently see one-, two-, and sometimes three-sentence paragraphs in a newspaper, but newspapers arbitrarily break up paragraphs into small units merely to facilitate reading. In the narrow columns of a newspaper, a five- or six-sentence paragraph would look forbiddingly dense. So the short paragraph is a convention used by all newspapers.

Judgment about whether a paragraph is adequately developed is, of course, a relative matter. Because some ideas need more development than others, no one can say how many sentences a paragraph needs to be adequately developed. Each paragraph must be judged on its own terms and in the context in which it appears. If a paragraph has a topic sentence, for instance, that sentence can dictate how long the paragraph needs to be. What was done in the previous paragraph and what will be done in the paragraph that follows may dictate how long the middle paragraph needs to be.

Three samples of inadequately developed paragraphs will be displayed, and after each paragraph has been discussed, it will be presented in a revised version:

1. The government has resorted to many methods of preventing tax frauds. Most of these methods have proved ineffective so far.

This sample paragraph and the two that follow have all been taken out of context, but even so, we can sense the inadequate development of these skimpy paragraphs.

Paragraph **1**, for instance, raises some expectations that are not satisfied. The first sentence mentions **many methods**, and we expect that the next sentence will go on to specify at least one of those many methods. Instead, the writer changes the subject: we are now told that these methods (unspecified) have proved ineffective. First of all, the writer has to decide whether he or she wants this paragraph to specify the many methods that the government has used to prevent tax frauds or whether it is preferable to show how or why the methods proved ineffective. Having settled on the topic of the paragraph, the writer can then make some decisions about how to develop the paragraph and how much to develop it.

Here is a revision of paragraph **1**:

52

1. Most of the methods that the government has resorted to in order to prevent tax frauds have proved ineffective. For instance, the government tried the system of requiring restaurant owners to report not only the salaries of waiters but also the amount of their daily tips. The waiters, of course, circumvented that system by never reporting the correct total of their tips. Cabdrivers, bellhops, doormen, and others whose chief source of income is tips are a problem too. The government tried setting a standard tip-per-transaction, but these employees rarely reported the correct number of customers they had served, and there was no way that the government could reliably check the figures that were reported. Those who are self-employed constitute the major problem for the Internal Revenue Service. All efforts to get the self-employed to keep and to report accurate or honest records of business transactions have proven futile. It seems that if they are determined enough and smart enough they can evade even the most ingenious efforts of the IRS to make them pay all the taxes that they should pay.

(expanded by giving examples)

Here is the second example of a thinly developed paragraph:

2. The young people now growing up in this drug-oriented atmosphere should be made aware of the disadvantages of their indulging in drugs, just as the young people of the previous generation were cautioned about the disadvantages of their engaging in premarital sex. In both cases, responsibility for one's actions is the chief lesson to be taught.

Even if paragraph **2** were a summary paragraph that followed a paragraph (or several paragraphs) in which the writer had discussed the disadvantages of indulging in drugs, the reader could reasonably expect the writer to say something more about the notion presented in the second sentence. What kind of legal or moral responsibilities do drug-users have to themselves? What kind of responsibilities do they have to their family and to society in general? Once they have been "hooked," can they still be held responsible for their actions? What are the consequences, for themselves and for society, of their refusing to be responsible for their actions? These questions suggest ways in which the writer might have expanded the thinly developed paragraph.

Here is one way in which that thinly developed paragraph might have been expanded:

2. Young people who indulge in drugs should be made aware of their responsibilities for their actions. They must be taught that an insatiable appetite for drugs has consequences not only for themselves but also for family, friends, and society. Parents are the ones who are hurt the most by a son or daughter who gets hooked on drugs. They suffer deeply when they see someone they love become a slave to drugs; and they also feel ashamed and guilt-ridden for their child's addiction. Friends too suffer anguish and humiliation; but they suffer most from the loss of the companionship of a former friend. The effects on society

are too numerous to specify completely, but they include the dangers from an addict's resort to violent crimes, the cost of maintaining special police forces, and the loss of a valuable contributing member to the community. Drug-users don't just run the risk of ruining their own lives; they can affect the lives of dozens of other people.

(expanded by pointing out the effects or consequences of a situation)

Here is the third sample of an inadequately developed paragraph:

3. Before we seek answers to those questions, however, we should settle on a definition of the term *illiteracy*. For most people, *illiteracy* signifies the inability to read and write.

A reader may feel that paragraph **3** is developed as much as it needs to be. The writer has suggested the need for a definition of the term **illiteracy** and in the next sentence has provided a definition of the term. But even lacking the context of both the paragraph that went before and the paragraph that came after this one, we can judge this paragraph to be inadequately developed. The mere fact that the writer felt the need to seek a definition of a principal term before going on with the discussion indicates that the writer recognized the slipperiness of the term. The phrase that begins the second sentence, **For most people**, suggests that regardless of the common meaning of **illiteracy** (an inability to read and write), the term has other meanings for other people. What the reader expects to get in this paragraph and doesn't get is an exposition of the word's complex meanings. Refining the definition of the word **illiteracy** is one of the ways of expanding the paragraph:

3. Before we seek answers to those questions, however, we should settle on a definition of the term *illiteracy*. For most people, *illiteracy* signifies a person's inability to read and write. But that

52

general definition does not reveal the wide range of disabilities covered by the term. There are those who cannot read or write anything in their native language. Others can read minimally, but they cannot write anything—not even their own names. A large number of people have minimal skills in reading and writing, but they cannot apply those skills to some of the ordinary tasks of day-to-day living—e.g., they cannot make sense of the written instructions on a can of weed-killer or fill out an application form. Such people are sometimes referred to as being "functionally illiterate." So whenever we discuss the problem of illiteracy with others, we should make sure what degree of disability people have in mind when they use the term *illiteracy.*

(expanded by defining or explaining a key term)

52

The first step in developing a paragraph is to consider its central idea—whether that is expressed in a topic sentence or merely implied—and determine what that idea commits you to do. It sometimes helps to ask yourself questions like those that were asked above about the second sample paragraph. If such questioning establishes what you are committed to do in a paragraph, you can then make a choice of the appropriate means of developing the paragraph. Here is a list of the common ways in which writers develop their paragraphs:

(a) They present examples or illustrations of what they are discussing.

(b) They cite data—facts, statistics, evidence, details, precedents—that corroborate or confirm what they are discussing.

(c) They quote, paraphrase, or summarize the testimony of others about what they are discussing.

(d) They relate an anecdote or event that has some bearing on what they are discussing.

(e) They define terms connected with what they are discussing.

(f) They compare or contrast what they are discussing with something else—usually something familiar to the readers—and point out similarities or differences.

(g) They explore the causes or reasons for the phenomenon or situation they are discussing.

(h) They point out the effects or consequences of the phenomenon or situation they are discussing.

(i) They explain how something operates.

(j) They describe the person, place, or thing they are discussing.

52

In the revisions of the examples of inadequately developed paragraphs, we have seen how one or other of these means of development was used to expand the paragraphs. If we inspect other well-developed paragraphs, we will find that these, and maybe other, means of development were used to flesh out the paragraphs.

PUNCTUATION

Graphic punctuation, which is the only kind dealt with in this section, is a feature of the written language exclusively. For the written language, it performs the kinds of function that intonation (pitch, stress, pause, and juncture) performs for the spoken language. Punctuation and intonation can be considered as part of the grammar of a language because they join with other grammatical devices (word order, inflections, and function words) to help convey meaning. If writers would regard punctuation as an integral—and often indispensable—part of the expressive system of a language, they might cease to think of it as just another nuisance imposed on them by editors and English teachers.

In *Structural Essentials of English* (New York: Harcourt Brace Jovanovich, 1956), Harold Whitehall has neatly summarized the four main functions of graphic punctuation:

- **For LINKING parts of sentences and words.**
  semicolon **;**
  colon **:**
  dash ——
  hyphen (for words only) **-**

● **For SEPARATING sentences and parts of sentences.**

period **.**
question mark **?**
exclamation point **!**
comma **,**

● **For ENCLOSING parts of sentences.**

pair of commas **,** . . . **,**
pair of dashes —— . . . ——
pair of parentheses **(** . . . **)**
pair of brackets **[** . . . **]**
pair of quotation marks **"** . . . **"**

● **For INDICATING omissions.**

apostrophe (e.g., **don't, we'll, it's, we've**)
period (e.g., abbreviations, **Mrs., U.S., A.H. Robinson**)
dash (e.g., **John R–, D–n!**)
triple periods (**.** . . to indicate omitted words in a quotation)

Punctuation is strictly a convention. There is no reason in the nature of things why the mark **?** should be used in English to indicate a question. The Greek language, for instance, uses **;** (what we call a semicolon) to mark questions. Nor is there any reason in the nature of things why the single comma should be a separating device rather than a linking device. It is usage that has established the distinctive functions of the various marks of punctuation. And although styles of punctuation have changed somewhat from century to century and even from country to country, the conventions of punctuation set forth in the following section are the current conventions in the United States. Although publishers of newspapers, magazines, and books often have style manuals that prescribe, for their own editors and writers, a style of punctuation that may differ in some particulars from the prevailing conventions, writers who observe the conventions of punctuation set forth in this section can rest assured that they are following the predominant system in the United States.

60 Comma, Compound Sentence

Put a comma in front of the coordinating conjunction that joins the independent clauses of a compound sentence.

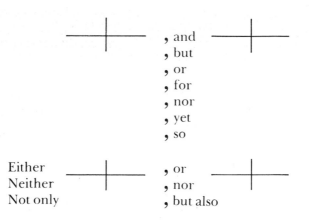

Examples of compound sentences that need a comma:

1. He disliked this kind of cruel humor yet he continued to tease her unmercifully.

rewrite:

He disliked this kind of cruel humor, yet he continued to tease her unmercifully.

2. Alice's embarrassment amused Julian so he deliberately pursued the conversation with the Dirty Old Man across the aisle.

rewrite:

Alice's embarrassment amused Julian, so he deliberately pursued the conversation with the Dirty Old Man across the aisle.

3. He returned the book for his mother refused to pay any more fines.

rewrite:

He returned the book, for his mother refused to pay any more fines.

4. The decision about whether to attend college should be left entirely to the children and their parents should make every effort to reconcile themselves to the decision.

rewrite:

The decision about whether to attend college should be left entirely to the children, and their parents should make every effort to reconcile themselves to the decision.

60

5. It was snowing outside and in the building Kazuko felt safe.

rewrite:

It was snowing outside, and in the building Kazuko felt safe.

6. Either the senators will reject the proposal or they will modify it in such a way as to make it innocuous.

rewrite:

Either the senators will reject the proposal, or they will modify it in such a way as to make it innocuous.

This convention of the comma comes into play only in compound sentences (sentences composed of two or more independent clauses) or in compound-complex sentences (sentences composed of two or more independent clauses and at least one dependent clause). According to **62**, pairs of words, phrases, or clauses (except independent clauses) joined by one of the coordinating conjunctions should *not* be separated with a comma.

This practice of using a comma probably developed because in many compounded sentences, the absence of the comma could lead to an initial misreading of the sentence. In sentence **3**, for instance, it would be quite natural for us to read **for** as a preposition and consequently to read the sentence this way: **He returned the book for his mother** . . . . But when we came to the verb **refused**, we would realize that we had misread the syntax of the sentence, and we would have to back up and reread the sentence. Likewise, in sentence **4**, we tend to read the sentence in this way: . . . **should be left entirely to the children and their parents** . . . . But when we read on, we realize that the absence of a comma before the conjunction **and** has trapped us into a misreading of the syntax of the sentence. A comma placed before the coordinating conjunction that joins the independent clauses of a compound sentence will prevent such misreadings.

Some handbooks authorize you to omit this separating comma under certain conditions. However, if you *invariably* insert a comma before the coordinating conjunction that joins the independent clauses, you never have to pause to consider whether those conditions are present, and you can be confident that your sentence will always be read correctly the first time. So the safest practice is *always* to insert the comma before the coordinating conjunction or before the second of the correlative conjunctions (**either** . . . **or**; **neither** . . . **nor**; **not only** . . . **but also**) that join the main clauses of a compound or compound-complex sentence.

60

61   Comma, Introductory

Introductory words, phrases, or clauses should be separated from the main (independent) clause by a comma.

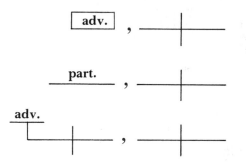

Examples of introductory words, phrases, and clauses that need a comma:

61

1. Underneath the papers were scorched.
   (*introductory word*)

rewrite:
   Underneath, the papers were scorched.

2. I tiptoed into the house. Inside the front room looked as though it had been recently painted by a group of three-year-olds.
   (*introductory word*)

rewrite:
   I tiptoed into the house. Inside, the front room looked as though it had been recently painted by a group of three-year-olds.

3. In addition to the logical errors Doris had made several miscalculations in addition and subtraction.
   (*introductory prepositional phrase*)

rewrite:

In addition to the logical errors, Doris had made several miscalculations in addition and subtraction.

4. As we went by the church revealed all of its redbrick Georgian elegance.
    (*introductory adverbial clause*)

    rewrite:

    As we went by, the church revealed all of its redbrick Georgian elegance.

5. After hurriedly gathering the crowd decided to rush the gates.
    (*introductory verbal phrase*)

    rewrite:

    After hurriedly gathering, the crowd decided to rush the gates.

6. Although she vehemently protested the violence was not as destructive as he predicted it would be.
    (*introductory adverbial clause*)

    rewrite:

    Although she vehemently protested, the violence was not as destructive as he predicted it would be.

61

The reason for the comma after introductory elements is that the comma facilitates the reading of the sentence and often prevents an initial misreading. Without the "protective" comma, the syntax of the six sample sentences above would probably be misread on the first reading. You probably read the sample sentences this way the first time:

1. **Underneath the papers** . . . .
2. **Inside the front room** . . . .
3. **In addition to the logical errors [that] Doris had made** . . . .
4. **As we went by the church** . . . .
5. **After hurriedly gathering the crowd** . . . .
6. **Although she vehemently protested the violence** . . . .

The insertion of a comma after each of these introductory elements would have prevented that kind of misreading.

Even in those instances, however, where there is little or no chance of an initial misreading, the insertion of a comma after the introductory word, phrase, or clause will facilitate the reading of the sentence. If you read the following sentences twice, the first time without the comma, the second time with the comma after the introductory word, phrase, or clause, you will discover that it is easier to read and understand the sentences that have a comma after the introductory element:

> Besides the crowd wasn't impressed by his flaming oratory.
>
> Having failed to impress the crowd with his flaming oratory he tried another tactic.
>
> After he saw that his flaming oratory had not impressed the crowd he tried another tactic.

If you *always* insert a comma after an introductory word, phrase, or clause, you will not have to consider each time whether it would be safe to omit the comma, and you can be confident that your sentence will not be misread.

62

62   No Comma, Coordinating Conjunction

Pairs of words, phrases, or dependent clauses joined by one of the coordinating conjunctions should not be separated with a comma.

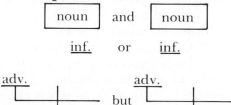

Examples of pairs incorrectly separated by a comma:

1. The mother, and the father appeared in court, and testified about their son's activities.

   (*two nouns and two verbs joined by **and***)

   rewrite:
   The mother and the father appeared in court and testified about their son's activities.

2. There was nothing they could do to prevent the gas attack, or to protect themselves against the gas once it had been released.

   (*two infinitive phrases joined by **or***)

   rewrite:
   There was nothing they could do to prevent the gas attack or to protect themselves against the gas once it had been released.

3. The men who are able to work, but who are not willing to work will not be eligible to receive monthly welfare checks.

   (*two adjective clauses joined by **but***)

   rewrite:
   The men who are able to work but who are not willing to work will not be eligible to receive monthly welfare checks.

4. Marian was happiest when she was free of her parents' scrutiny, or when she was working in her garden.

   (*two adverb clauses joined by **or***)

   rewrite:
   Marian was happiest when she was free of her parents' scrutiny or when she was working in her garden.

The principle behind this convention is that what has been joined by one means (the coordinating conjunction) should not then be separated by another means (the comma, a separating device). The function of the coordinating conjunction is to join units of equal rank (e.g., nouns with nouns, verbs with verbs, prepositional phrases with prepositional phrases, adjective clauses with adjective clauses). Once pairs of coordinate units have been joined by the conjunction, it makes no sense to separate them with a comma—as has been done in all the sample sentences above.

A pair of *independent* clauses is not covered by this rule. According to **60**, a comma should be inserted before the coordinating conjunction, because in this structure the omission of the comma could lead—and often does lead—to an initial misreading of the sentence. But there are almost no instances where the use of a comma would help the reading of pairs of words, phrases, or dependent clauses joined by a coordinating conjunction. As a matter of fact, sentence **1** is harder to read because of the comma that separates the two nouns of the subject (**mother** and **father**) and the two verbs of the predicate (**appeared** and **testified**). The commas used in that sentence only confuse the reader.

An exception to this convention occurs in the case of suspended structures, as in the following sentence:

62

> This account of an author's struggles with, and her anxieties about, her writing fascinated me.
>
> We must never relinquish our interest in, or our respect for, the accomplishments of our ancestors.

The phrases **struggles with** and **anxieties about** are called *suspended structures* because they are left "hanging" until the noun phrase **her writing**, which completes them grammatically, occurs. Likewise, the phrases **interest in** and **respect for** are "suspended" until they are completed by the phrase "the accomplishments of our ancestors."

Another exception to this convention occurs in the structure where the word or phrase following the word **or** presents not an alternative to the previous word or phrase (as in "right or wrong" and "fathers or mothers") but an *explanatory appositive* for the previous word or phrase. In such cases, the explanatory appositive is enclosed with a pair of commas, as in the following examples:

His fealty, or devotion, never wavered.

The holograph, or handwritten manuscript, was carefully examined by textual critics.

With these two exceptions, the joining device (the conjunction) and the separating device (the comma) should not work against one another.

63   Comma, Series

Use a comma to separate a series of coordinate words, phrases, or clauses.

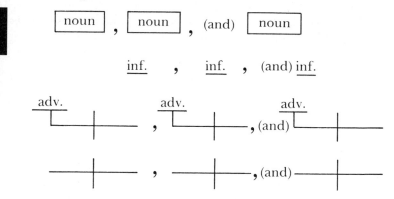

*(The parentheses around **and** in the diagrams indicate that the coordinating conjunction between the last two members of a series may sometimes be dispensed with. For instance, the phrasing **The tall, robust, gray-haired soldier rose to speak** is stylistically preferable to **The tall, robust, and gray-haired soldier rose to speak.**)*

Examples of series lacking one or more commas:

1. Could he cope with the challenges posed by war, poverty, pollution and crime?
   (*a series of nouns*)

rewrite:
   Could he cope with the challenges posed by war, poverty, pollution, and crime?

2. He would have to terminate the war, alleviate the plight of the poor, arrest the contamination of the environment and hobble the criminal.
   (*series of infinitive phrases, with* **to** *understood in the last three members of the series*)

rewrite:
   He would have to terminate the war, alleviate the plight of the poor, arrest the contamination of the environment, and hobble the criminal.

3. If she is willing to work if she is resourceful enough to formulate sensible policies if she subordinates her own interests to the interests of the community, she can rescue the nation from the despair that now prevails.
   (*series of adverb clauses*)

rewrite:
   If she is willing to work, if she is resourceful enough to formulate sensible policies, if she subordinates her own interests to the interests of the community, she can rescue the nation from the despair that now prevails.

63

4. She wanted to save the nation, she knew she could save it and eventually she did save it.
   (*series of independent clauses*)

rewrite:
   She wanted to save the nation, she knew she could save it, and eventually she did save it.

Whereas the convention stated in **62** says that *pairs* of coordinate words, phrases, or clauses should not be separated with a comma, the convention governing a *series* of coordinate words, phrases, and clauses says that these units should be separated with commas. (*A series is to be understood as a sequence of three or more coordinate units.*) Built on the principle of parallelism (see **27**), the series always involves words, phrases, or clauses of a similar kind. So a series should never couple dissimilar grammatical elements—for example, nouns with adjectives, prepositional phrases with infinitive phrases, adjective clauses with adverb clauses.

The convention that will be recommended here follows this formula:

a, b, and c.

Another acceptable formula for the series is

a, b and c

where no comma is used between the last two members of the series when they are joined by a coordinating conjunction. The formula **a, b, and c** is adopted here because the alternative formula (**a, b and c**) sometimes leads to ambiguity. Consider the following example, which uses the **a, b and c** formula:

> Please send me a gross each of the red, green, blue, orange and black ties.

The shipping clerk who received that order might wonder whether five gross of ties (**red**, **green**, **blue**, **orange**, **black**) were being ordered or only four gross (**red**, **green**, **blue**, **orange-and-black**). If five gross were being ordered, a comma after **orange** would specify the order unambiguously; if four gross were being ordered, hyphens should have been used to signify the combination of colors.

A more common instance of the ambiguity that is sometimes created by the use of the **a, b and c** formula is the following:

63

He appealed to the administrators, the deans and the chairpersons.

In this sentence, it is not clear whether he appealed to three different groups (**administrators**, **deans**, **chairpersons**)—a meaning that would have been clearly indicated by the **a, b, and c** formula—or to only one group, **administrators**, who are then specified in the two appositives **deans** and **chairpersons**.

Since there is never any chance of ambiguity if you use the **a, b, and c** formula, you would be well advised to adopt this option for punctuating a series.

64 Comma, Nonrestrictive

Nonrestrictive adjective clauses should be enclosed with a pair of commas.

Examples of nonrestrictive adjective clauses that should be enclosed with commas:

1. My oldest brother who is a chemist was hurt in an accident last week.

rewrite:

My oldest brother, who is a chemist, was hurt in an accident last week.

2. The shopkeeper caters only to American tourists who have enough money to buy what they want and to aristocratic families.

rewrite:
> The shopkeeper caters only to American tourists, who have enough money to buy what they want, and to aristocratic families.

3. Norman Mailer's book which most reviewers considered juvenile in its pronouncements was severely panned by feminist-movement groups.

rewrite:
> Norman Mailer's book, which most reviewers considered juvenile in its pronouncements, was severely panned by feminist-movement groups.

4. The townspeople threaten the strangers who are looking at the new car.

rewrite:
> The townspeople threaten the strangers, who are looking at the new car.

64 A nonrestrictive adjective clause is one that supplies information about the noun that it modifies but information that is not needed to identify or specify the particular person, place, or thing that is being talked about. (The four **that** clauses in this last sentence, for instance, are *restrictive* adjective clauses—clauses that supply *necessary* identifying or specifying information about the nouns that they modify.)

In sentence 1, the adjective clause **who is a chemist** supplies additional information about **my oldest brother**, but this information is not needed to identify which of the brothers was hurt in the accident, because the adjective **oldest** sufficiently identifies the brother being talked about.

One test to determine whether an adjective clause is nonrestrictive is to read the sentence without it, and if the particular person, place, or thing being talked about is sufficiently identified by what is left, the adjective clause can be considered nonrestrictive—and, according to the convention, should be marked off with enclosing commas. If, for instance, you were to drop the adjective clause from sentence **1** and say **My oldest brother was hurt in an accident last week**, your readers would not have to ask, "Which one of your brothers was hurt?" The brother that was hurt is specified by the adjective **oldest**, since there can be only one oldest brother. The clause **who is a chemist** merely supplies some additional but nonessential information about the oldest brother.

Another test to determine whether an adjective clause is nonrestrictive is the *intonation* test. Read these two written versions of sentence **2** aloud:

> He caters to American tourists, who have enough money to buy what they want, and to aristocratic families.
>
> He caters to American tourists who have enough money to buy what they want and to aristocratic families.

In reading the first sentence aloud, speakers of the language would pause briefly after the words **tourists** and **want** (that is, in the places where the commas are) and would lower the pitch of their voices slightly in enunciating the clause **who have enough money to buy what they want**. In reading the second sentence aloud, speakers would read right through without a pause and would not lower the pitch of their voices in reading the adjective clause.

In writing, it makes a *significant* difference whether the adjective clause in a sentence is marked off with commas or not. *With* the enclosing commas, sentence **2**, for instance, means this: He caters to American tourists (who, incidentally, usually have enough money to buy what they want) and to aristocratic families. *Without* the enclosing commas, the sentence means this: He caters only to those American tourists who have enough money to buy what they want (he doesn't cater to any American tourists who don't have

64

enough money to buy) and to aristocratic families. Those two meanings are quite different from one another, and for that reason, it is extremely important, in a written text, whether or not the adjective clause is marked off with commas.

Likewise, it is important whether or not the adjective clause in sentence **4** is marked off with a comma. Without the comma before the **who** clause, the sentence means that the townspeople threaten only those strangers who are looking at the new car (with the implication that some are not looking at it). But if the writer wants to say that the townspeople threaten *all* the strangers—all of whom are looking enviously at the new car—he or she should have put a comma before the **who** clause, thus indicating that this adjective clause is to be read as a nonrestrictive clause.

64

There are some instances in which the adjective clause is almost invariably nonrestrictive:

(a) Where the antecedent is a **proper noun**, the adjective clause is usually nonrestrictive:

> Martin Chuzzlewit, who is a character in Dickens' novel, . . .
>
> New York City, which has the largest urban population in the United States, . . .
>
> The College of William and Mary, which was founded in 1693, . . .

(b) Where, in the nature of things, there could be **only one such** person, place, or thing, the adjective clause is usually nonrestrictive:

> My mother, who is now forty-six years old, . . .
>
> Their birthplace, which is Jamestown, . . .
>
> His fingerprints, which are on file in Washington, . . .

(c) Where the identity of the antecedent has been clearly established by the **previous context**, the adjective clause is usually nonrestrictive:

My brother, who has hazel eyes, . . . (where it is clear from the context that you have only one brother or where you have specified which one you are talking about)

The book, which never made the bestseller list, . . . (where the previous sentence has identified the particular book being talked about)

Such revolutions, which never enlist the sympathies of the majority of the people, . . . (where the kinds of revolutions being talked about have been specified in the previous sentences or paragraphs)

Which is the usual relative pronoun that introduces non-restrictive adjective clauses. **That** is the more common relative pronoun used in restrictive adjective clauses. **Who** (or its inflected forms **whose** and **whom**) is the usual relative pronoun when the antecedent is a person; **that**, however, may also be used when the antecedent is a person and the clause is restrictive: either "the men whom I admire" or "the men that I admire."

65

65 No Comma, Restrictive

Restrictive adjective clauses should not be marked off with a pair of commas.

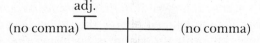

Examples of adjective clauses that should not be marked off with a pair of commas:

1. Middle-aged people, who have slow reflexes, should be denied a driver's license.

rewrite:

Middle-aged people who have slow reflexes should be denied a driver's license.

2. The poem is about a girl, who has been in Vietnam and has rejoined her family.

rewrite:

The poem is about a girl who has been in Vietnam and has rejoined her family.

3. All streets, alleys, and thoroughfares, that are in the public domain, should be maintained by the city.

rewrite:

All streets, alleys, and thoroughfares that are in the public domain should be maintained by the city.

65

A restrictive adjective clause is one that identifies or specifies the particular person, place, or thing being talked about. It "restricts" the noun that it modifies; it "defines"—that is, "draws boundaries around"—the noun being talked about. Nonrestrictive clauses, as we saw in **64**, give *additional* information about the nouns that they modify, but they do not serve the *identify* or *specify* the noun that they modify.

In sentence **1**, the adjective clause **who have slow reflexes** is restrictive because it identifies, defines, designates, specifies *which* middle-aged people should be denied a driver's license. The writer of that sentence did not intend to say that *all* middle-aged people should be denied a driver's license, but with the commas enclosing the adjective clause, the sentence does suggest that all of them should not be allowed to drive. The writer probably meant to say that only those middle-aged people who have slow reflexes should be denied a driver's license. Leaving out the enclosing commas will make the sentence say what the writer intended to say.

The commas in sentences 2 and 3 should also be omitted. The **who** clause in sentence 2 "restricts" the kind of girl that the poem is about. If the commas enclosing the **that** clause in sentence 3 are omitted, the sentence will say what the writer obviously intended to say: that the city is responsible for maintaining only those streets, alleys, and thoroughfares that are in the public domain.

If you were speaking those three sentences, your voice would do what the presence or the absence of the commas does. If the commas are left out—as they should be—your voice would join the adjective clause to the noun or nouns that it modifies by running on without a pause after the nouns. With the commas, your voice would pause momentarily at those junctures, and a different meaning would be conveyed.

According to the convention, nonrestrictive adjective clauses modifying nonhuman nouns should be introduced with the relative pronoun **which**, and restrictive adjective clauses modifying nonhuman nouns should be introduced with the relative pronoun **that**:

> Governments, which are instituted to protect the rights of men, should be responsive to the will of the people.
> (*nonrestrictive*)
>
> Governments that want to remain in favor with their constituents must be responsive to the will of the people.
> (*restrictive*)

Here is another distinctive fact about the phrasing of restrictive and nonrestrictive clauses: the relative pronoun may sometimes be omitted in restrictive clauses, but it may never be omitted in nonrestrictive clauses. Note that it is impossible in English to drop the relative pronouns **who** and **whom** from the following nonrestrictive clauses:

> John, who is my dearest friend, won't drink with me.
> John, whom I love dearly, hardly notices me.

(In the first sentence, however, the clause **who is my dearest friend** could be reduced to an appositive phrase: **John, *my dearest friend*, won't drink with me.**)

In restrictive adjective clauses, we sometimes have the option of using or not using the relative pronoun:

> The one whom I love dearly hardly notices me.
> (*with the relative pronoun*)
>
> The one that I love dearly hardly notices me.
> (*with the relative pronoun*)
>
> The one I love dearly hardly notices me.
> (*without the relative pronoun*)

65

In restrictive adjective clauses like these, where the relative pronoun serves as the object of the verb of the adjective clause, the relative pronoun may be omitted. The relative pronoun in restrictive clauses may also be omitted if it serves as the object of a preposition in the adjective clause: "The man I gave the wallet to disappeared" (here the understood *whom* or *that* serves as the object of the preposition **to**). However, the relative pronoun may *not* be omitted when it serves as the subject of the restrictive adjective clause:

> He who exalts himself shall be humbled.
> (***who*** *cannot be omitted*)
>
> The money that was set aside for scholarships was squandered on roads.
> (***that*** *cannot be omitted*)

You should learn the difference between restrictive and nonrestrictive clauses because the meaning of a sentence can change radically if commas are put in where they should not be or if they are omitted where they should be.

66   Semicolon, Compound Sentence

If the independent clauses of a compound sentence are not joined by one of the coordinating conjunctions, they should be joined by a semicolon.

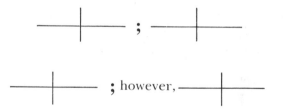

Examples of compound sentences that should be joined by a semicolon:

1. This refutation is based on an appeal to reason however, one must remember that an emotional appeal can also move people to reject an argument.

rewrite:

   This refutation is based on an appeal to reason; however, one must remember that an emotional appeal can also move people to reject an argument.

2. All the students spontaneously supported the team, they wanted to show their loyalty, even though they were disappointed with the outcome of the game.

rewrite:

> All the students spontaneously supported the team; they wanted to show their loyalty, even though they were disappointed with the outcome of the game.

3. She loved her father, in fact, she practically worshipped him.

rewrite:

> She loved her father; in fact, she practically worshipped him.

The coordinating conjunctions are **and**, **but**, **or**, **nor**, **for**, **yet**, **so**. In the absence of one of those words, the independent clauses of a compound sentence should be spliced together with a punctuation device: the semicolon.

Words and phrases like **however**, **therefore**, **then**, **indeed**, **nevertheless**, **consequently**, **thus**, **moreover**, **furthermore**, **in fact**, **on the other hand**, **on the contrary** are not coordinating conjunctions; they are called *conjunctive adverbs*. Conjunctive adverbs provide logical links between sentences and between parts of sentences, but they do not function as grammatical splicers. Unlike coordinating conjunctions, which must always be placed *between* the two elements they join, conjunctive adverbs enjoy some freedom of movement in the sentence.

In sentence **1**, the word **however** is placed between the two independent clauses, but evidence that this conjunctive adverb is not serving as the grammatical splicer of the two clauses is provided by the fact that **however** can be shifted to another position in the sentence: **This refutation is based on an appeal to reason; one must remember, however, that an emotional appeal can also move people to reject an argument.** The coordinating conjunction **but**, on the other hand, which is equivalent in meaning to **however**, could occupy no other position in the sentence than *between* the end of the first clause (after the word **reason**) and the beginning of the next clause (before the word **one**).

Nor can the independent clauses of a compound sentence be joined by a comma, because the comma is a separating device, not a joining device. Compound sentences so punctuated—like sentence **2**—are called **comma splices** (see **30**). As indicated in **60**, if a compound sentence is joined by one of the coordinating conjunctions, a comma should be put in front of the conjunction to mark off the end of one independent clause and the beginning of the next independent clause. But whenever a coordinating conjunction is not present to joint the independent clauses, a semicolon must be used to join them. The semicolon serves both to mark the division between the two clauses and to join them.

Sometimes it is advisable to use both a semicolon and a coordinating conjunction to join the independent clauses of a compound sentence. When the clauses are unusually long and have commas within them, a semicolon placed before the coordinating conjunction helps to signal the end of one clause and the beginning of the next one, as in this example:

66

> Struggling to salvage what was left of the semester, he pleaded with his English teacher, who was notoriously softhearted, to grant him an extension of time on his written assignments, quizzes, and class reports; **but** he forgot that, even with the best of intentions, he had only so many hours every day when he could study and only a limited reserve of energy.

The coordinating conjunction **but** serves to join the two main clauses of the compound sentence, but the use of the semicolon in addition to the conjunction makes it easier to read the sentence.

67 Semicolon, Independent Clauses

Whenever you use a semicolon, be sure that you have an independent clause on both sides of the semicolon.

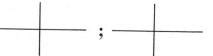

Examples of failure to observe this convention:

1. She played the guitar expertly; although she couldn't read a note of music.

rewrite:

She played the guitar expertly, although she couldn't read a note of music.

2. Americans spend far too many hours as spectators of sports instead of as participants in them; watching meaningless drivel on television instead of spending that time reading a book.

rewrite:

Americans spend far too many hours as spectators of sports instead of as participants in them; they spend far too many hours watching meaningless drivel on television instead of spending that time reading a book.

3. The two series of poems also differ in style; the *Songs of Experience* being more vague and complex than the *Songs of Innocence.*

rewrite:

The two series of poems also differ in style, the *Songs of Experience* being more vague and complex than the *Songs of Innocence.*

4. An industry like this benefits everyone, from the poor, for whom it creates employment; to the rich, who are made richer by it.

rewrite:

> An industry like this benefits everyone, from the poor, for whom it creates employment, to the rich, who are made richer by it.

This convention is the corollary of **66**. It cautions against using the semicolon to join elements of unequal rank. Accordingly, if there is an independent clause on one side of the semicolon, there must be a balancing independent clause on the other side.

In all of the examples above, a semicolon has been used to join units of *unequal* rank. In all four sentences, there is an independent clause on the *left-hand* side of the semicolon; however, there is no independent clause on the *right-hand* side of the semicolon in any of those sentences. What is on the right-hand side of the semicolon could be called a sentence fragment (see **29**).

In sentence **1**, there is the independent clause **she played the guitar expertly** on the left-hand side of the semicolon, but on the right-hand side of the semicolon, there is only the adverb clause **although she couldn't read a note of music**. That adverb clause belongs with, depends on, the first clause. Since it is an integral part of the first clause, it should be *joined* with that clause. The effect of the semicolon is to make the adverb clause part of *another* clause that begins after the semicolon. But on the right-hand side of the semicolon, there is no independent clause that the subordinate, dependent adverb clause can be a part of. One way to correct the sentence is to supply an independent clause, on the right-hand side of the semi-colon, that the adverb clause can adhere to—e.g., **She played the guitar expertly; although she couldn't read a note of music, she simply had a knack for playing stringed instruments.** The other way to correct the sentence is to substitute a comma for the semicolon.

67

Sentences **2**, **3**, and **4** could also be corrected by substituting a comma for the semicolon, as shown. But in **2**, it would probably be better to supply an independent clause on the right-hand side of the semicolon. So revised, the sentence would have an independent clause on *both* sides of the semicolon.

68   Colon, for Lead-in

Use a colon after a grammatically complete lead-in sentence that formally announces a subsequent enumeration, specification, illustration, or extended quotation.

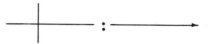

68

The following sentences either need a colon or use a colon improperly:

1. The courses I am taking this quarter are: English, sociology, economics, political science, and psychology.

rewrite:

The courses I am taking this quarter are as follows: English, sociology, economics, political science, and psychology. (*an enumeration*)

2. His approach works like this—after displaying his product and extolling its virtues, he asks the homemaker for a small rug that needs cleaning.

rewrite:

His approach works like this: after displaying his product and extolling its virtues, he asks the homemaker for a small rug that needs cleaning. (*an illustration*)

3. Examples of the diction used to evoke the horror of the scene include vivid images like: "coughing like hags," "thick green light," "guttering," "white eyes writhing in his face," "gargling from froth-corrupted lungs."

rewrite:

Examples of the diction used to evoke the horror of the scene include vivid images like these: "coughing like hags," "thick green light," "guttering," "white eyes writhing in his face," "gargling from froth-corrupted lungs." (*an enumeration*)

4. The reaction of the crowd signified only one thing, apathy.

rewrite:

The reaction of the crowd signified only one thing: apathy. (*a specification*)

A colon signals that what *follows* it is a spelling out, a detailing of what was formally announced in the clause on the left-hand side of the colon. What distinguishes the colon from the dash as a symbolic device is that the colon throws the reader's attention *forward,* whereas the dash as a linking device throws the reader's attention *backward* (see **69**). Although a word, a phrase, or a clause or a series of words, phrases, or clauses can follow the colon, there must be an independent clause (a grammatically complete sentence) on the left-hand side of the colon.

68

In accord with this principle, sentence 1 should not have been punctuated the way it was; that punctuation makes no more sense than punctuating a sentence in this way:

My name is: John Adams.

In both cases, the words following the colon are needed to complete the sentence grammatically. So either the colon must be dropped altogether, or enough words must be added to make the clause on the left-hand side of the colon a grammatically complete sentence—in sentence **1**, for instance, put **these** or **as follows** after the verb **are**.

In sentence **3**, the quoted phrases following the colon are needed to complete the prepositional phrase that begins with **like**. Therefore, either drop the colon or add a completing word like **these** before the colon. Since the lead-in clause in sentence **2** throws the reader's attention forward, the dash after **this** should be replaced by a colon. Likewise, the comma in the fourth sentence should be replaced by a colon.

A colon is conventionally used after the lead-in sentence that introduces an extended quotation in a research paper. Here is an example of that use:

> Toward the end of the preface, Dr. Johnson confessed that he abandoned his earlier expectation that his dictionary would be able to "fix the language":
>
>> Those who have been persuaded to think well of my design will require that it should fix our language and put a stop to those alterations which time and chance have hitherto been suffered to make in it without opposition. With this consequence I will confess that I flattered myself for a while, but now begin to fear that I have indulged expectation which neither reason nor experience can justify.

69 Dash, for Summation

Use a dash when the word or word-group that follows it constitutes a summation, an amplification, or a reversal of what went before it.

Examples of sentences that need to be punctuated with a dash:

1. English, psychology, history, and philosophy, these were the courses I took last quarter.

rewrite:

English, psychology, history, and philosophy—these were the courses I took last quarter. (*a summation*)

2. If he was pressured, he would become sullen and tight-lipped, a reaction that did not endear him to the president of the Senate.

rewrite:

If he was pressured, he would become sullen and tight-lipped—a reaction that did not endear him to the president of the Senate. (*a summation*)

3. Time and time again, she would admit that she should have realized her mistakes, that she should have read the danger signs more accurately, that she should have heeded the advice of her friends, and then go ahead with her original plans.

rewrite:

Time and time again, she would admit that she should have realized her mistakes, that she should have read the danger signs more accurately, that she should have heeded the advice of her friends—and then go ahead with her original plans. (*a reversal*)

69

Unlike the colon (see **68**), which directs the reader's attention forward, the dash usually directs the reader's attention backward. What follows the dash, when it is used as a linking device, looks back to what preceded it for the particulars or details that spell out the meaning or invest the meaning with pungency or irony.

The colon and the dash are usually not interchangeable marks of punctuation. They signal a different relationship between the word-groups that precede them and those that follow them. After much practice in writing, one develops a sense for the subtle distinction in relationships signaled by the punctuation in the following sentences:

The reaction of the crowd signified only one thing: apathy.

The people clearly indicated their indifference to the provocative speech—an apathy that later came back to haunt them.

In the first sentence, the lead-in clause before the colon clearly alerts the reader to expect a specification of what is hinted at in that clause. In the second sentence, there is no such alerting of the reader in the lead-in clause; but following the dash, there is an unexpected commentary on what was said in the lead-in clause, a summary commentary that forces the reader to look backward and that receives a special emphasis by being set off with a dash. The colon and the single dash are both linking devices, but they signal different kinds of thought relationships between parts of the sentence. Frequently, the dash signals a less formal relationship than the colon does.

You should avoid using the dash as a catchall mark of punctuation, one that is indiscriminately substituted for periods, commas, semicolons, etc.

70   Dash, Parenthetical Elements

Use a pair of dashes to enclose abrupt parenthetical elements that occur within a sentence.

— ... —

Examples of parenthetical elements that should be enclosed with a pair of dashes:

1. In some instances, although no one will admit it, the police overreacted to the provocation.

rewrite:
   In some instances—although no one will admit it—the police overreacted to the provocation.

2. What surprised everyone when the measure came to a vote was the chairperson's reluctance, indeed, downright refusal, to allow any riders to be attached to the bill.

rewrite:
What surprised everyone when the measure came to a vote was the chairperson's reluctance—indeed, downright refusal—to allow any riders to be attached to the bill.

3. Their unhappiness is due to the ease with which envy is aroused and to the difficulty, or should I say impossibility, of fighting against it.

rewrite:
Their unhappiness is due to the ease with which envy is aroused and to the difficulty—or should I say impossibility?—of fighting against it.

4. Yet despite the similarities in their travelogues (for indeed the same trip inspired both works), the two reports differ in some key aspects.

rewrite:
Yet despite the similarities in their travelogues—for indeed the same trip inspired both works—the two reports differ in some key aspects.

70

The three devices used to set off parenthetical elements in written prose are commas, parentheses, and dashes. The kind of parenthetical element that should be enclosed with a pair of dashes is the kind that interrupts the normal syntactical flow of the sentence. What characterizes all of the parenthetical elements in the examples above is that they abruptly arrest the normal flow of the sentence to add some qualifying or rectifying comment. The rhetorical effect of the enclosing dashes is to alert the reader to the interruption and thereby to help the reader understand the sentence.

A pair of parentheses is another typographical device used to mark off parenthetical elements in a sentence. Enclosure within parentheses is used mainly for those elements that merely add information or identification, as in sentences like these:

> All the companies that used the service were charged a small fee (usually $500) and were required to sign a contract (an "exclusive-use" agreement).

> The manager of each franchise is expected to report monthly to NARM (National Association of Retail Merchants) and to "rotate" (take turns doing various jobs) every two weeks.

The typographical device used to set off the mildest kind of interrupting element is a pair of commas. Whether to enclose a parenthetical element with commas or with parentheses or with dashes is often more a matter of stylistic choice than a matter of grammatical necessity. There are degrees of interruption and emphasis, and with practice, a writer develops an instinct for knowing when to mark off parenthetical elements with commas (lowest degree of interruption and emphasis), when to mark them off with parentheses (middle degree), and when to mark them off with dashes (highest degree). Consider the degrees of interruption and emphasis in the following sentences:

> That agency, as we have since learned, reported the incident directly to the Department of Justice.

> During the postwar years (at least from 1946 to 1952), no one in the agency dared challenge a directive from higher up.

> When the order was challenged, the attorney general—some claim it was his wife—put a call through to the president.

After much practice in writing, you will eventually learn how to detect the differences in degree of interruption and emphasis.

71 Formation of Dash

A dash is made on the typewriter with two unspaced hyphens and with no space before the dash or after the dash. (In handwriting, the dash should be made slightly longer than a hyphen.)

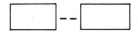

Because a typewriter does not have a separate key for a dash, you have to make a dash with two hyphens. Do not hit the spacebar on the typewriter *before* the first hyphen, *between* the first and second hyphen, or *after* the second hyphen. In short, do not hit the spacebar at all in forming the dash on the typewriter. When you are handwriting a text, you have to distinguish a dash from a hyphen by making the dash slightly longer than the hyphen.

Here is an illustration of the proper way to form the dash on the typewriter:

```
She forgot--if she ever knew--the functions

of the various marks of punctuation.
```

Here are some incorrect ways of forming the dash on a typewriter:

```
forgot-if            forgot - if
forgot -- if         forgot - - if
```

71

MECHANICS

The graphic devices dealt with in this section might be, and often are, classified as punctuation. But because such graphic devices as italics, capitalization, and numbers are not correlated—as punctuation marks are—with the intonational patterns of the spoken language, these devices are grouped in a separate section under the heading Mechanics. In the spoken language, a word printed with an initial capital letter is pronounced no differently from the same word printed with an initial lower-case letter. Nor is the italicized title of a book pronounced any differently from that same title printed without italics. (Italics used for emphasizing a word or phrase, however, do correspond to stress in the spoken language.) Even quotation marks, which we might regard as correlated with the spoken language, do not correspond to anything the voice does when it quotes direct speech.

But whether we classify these graphic devices as punctuation or as mechanics is immaterial. What is important to remember is that these devices are part of the written language exclusively and that they facilitate the reading of that language. Most readers would have at least momentary difficulty making sense of the following string of words:

Jill cried buckets as many as you can fetch Jack thought I don't have to please you over there she continued nuts pails they're called yelled Jack

If the proper punctuation and mechanics were used with that string of words, readers would be spared the momentary difficulty:

Jill cried, "Buckets! As many as you can fetch!" Jack thought, "I don't have to!" "Please, you over there!" she continued. "Nuts! *pails* they're called!" yelled Jack.

Deprived of the resources that the human voice possesses to clarify the meaning of words as spoken, you should be eager to use all those typographical devices that make it easier for your readers to grasp what you are trying to convey.

80   Quotation Mark, Period and Comma

The period or the comma always goes inside the closing quotation mark.

80

,"   ."

Examples of sentences with misplaced quotation marks:

1. The author announces at the beginning of her article that she is going to cite only "facts".

rewrite:

The author announces at the beginning of her article that she is going to cite only "facts."

2. "I know," she said, "that you are telling me a barefaced lie."

rewrite:

   "I know," she said, "that you are telling me a barefaced lie."

3. Bruce Springsteen's "head-banded, jean-clad fans", many of whom had traveled over a thousand miles to the concert, represented an aggregation of straight-A students.

rewrite:

   Bruce Springsteen's "head-banded, jean-clad fans," many of whom had traveled over a thousand miles to the concert, represented an aggregation of straight-A students.

This is a clear case where usage, rather than logic, has established the prevailing convention. Many reputable British editors and publishers put the period or comma *outside* the closing quotation mark, especially when the quotation marks enclose something less than a complete sentence—e.g., a word or a phrase, such as in sentences **1** and **3** above. But the American convention is almost universally to put the period or comma *inside* the closing quotation mark.

The advantage of such consistency is that you never have to pause and ask yourself, "Is this a case where the period goes inside or outside the quotation mark?" Whether it is a single word or a phrase or a dependent clause or an independent clause, the period or comma always goes *inside* the closing quotation mark.

In handwriting or in typewriting, take care to put the period or comma *clearly* inside the quotation mark, not *under* it, as in sentence **2**. In the case of a quotation within a quotation, both the single-stroke quotation mark and the double-stroke quotation mark go *outside* the period or the commas, as in this example:

   "I read recently," he said, "that Patrick Henry never said, 'Give me liberty or give me death.' "

80

81 Quotation Mark, Colon and Semicolon

The colon or semicolon always goes outside the closing quotation mark.

”:   ”;

Examples of a misplaced colon or semicolon in relation to the closing quotation mark:

1. She called this schedule of activities her "load:" work, study, exercise, recreation, and sleep.

rewrite:
    She called this schedule of activities her "load": work, study, exercise, recreation, and sleep.

2. He told his taunters, "I refuse to budge;" his knees, however, were shaking even as he said those words.

rewrite:
    He told his taunters, "I refuse to budge"; his knees, however, were shaking even as he said those words.

Whereas the period or the comma always goes *inside* the closing quotation mark, the colon or the semicolon always goes outside it. Whenever writers have occasion to use quotation marks with a colon or a semicolon, they have only to recall that the convention governing the relationship of the colon or the semicolon to the closing quotation mark is just the opposite of the convention for the period and the comma.

81

82   Quotation Mark, Question Mark

The question mark sometimes goes inside, sometimes outside, the closing quotation mark.

?"   "?

Examples of the question mark placed wrongly in relation to the closing quotation mark:

1. Who was it that said, "I regret that I have but one life to lose for my country?"

rewrite:
Who was it that said, "I regret that I have but one life to lose for my country"?

2. He asked her bluntly, "Will you marry me"?

rewrite:
He asked her bluntly, "Will you marry me?"

3. When will they stop asking, "Who then is responsible for the war"?

rewrite:
When will they stop asking, "Who then is responsible for the war?"

82

Although a period or a comma always goes inside the closing quotation mark and a colon or a semicolon always goes outside it, you have to consider each case individually before deciding whether to put the question mark inside or outside the closing quotation mark. Fortunately, the criteria for determining whether it goes inside or outside the quotation mark are fairly simple to apply:

(a) When the whole sentence, but not the unit enclosed in quotation marks, is a question, the question mark goes *outside* the closing quotation mark. (See sentence **1**.)

(b) When only the unit enclosed in quotation marks is a question, the question mark goes *inside* the closing quotation mark. (See sentence **2**.)

(c) When the whole sentence and the unit enclosed in quotation marks are both questions, the question mark goes *inside* the closing quotation mark. (See sentence **3**.)

Whenever the question mark occurs at the end of a sentence, it serves as the terminal punctuation for the entire sentence. In **(b)**, you do not add a period outside the closing quotation mark, and in **(c)**, you do not need to add another question mark outside the closing quotation mark.

83 Titles, Underlined

The titles of books, newspapers, magazines, professional journals, plays, long poems, movies, radio programs, television programs, long musical compositions, works of art, and the names of ships and airplanes should be *underlined*.

83

Examples of titles that should be underlined:

1. The critics have always rated Hemingway's "A Farewell to Arms" above his "For Whom the Bell Tolls."

rewrite:
    The critics have always rated Hemingway's <u>A Farewell to Arms</u> above his <u>For Whom the Bell Tolls</u>.
    (*underline the title of a book*)

2. To support her contention, she quoted a passage from an anonymous article in Newsweek.

rewrite:
    To support her contention, she quoted a passage from an anonymous article in <u>Newsweek</u>.
    (*underline the title of a magazine*)

3. My parents insisted on watching "All in the Family."
rewrite:
My parents insisted on watching <u>All in the Family</u>.
(*underline the title of a television show*)

4. Charles Darwin took a historic trip on the Beagle.
rewrite:
Charles Darwin took a historic trip on the <u>Beagle</u>.
(*underline the name of a ship*)

Printers use *italics*—a special typeface that slants slightly to the right—to set off certain words in a sentence (or certain sentences in a paragraph) from the body of words or sentences, which are printed in roman type (upright letters). The word *italics* in this and the previous sentence is printed in italics. In handwriting or typewriting, you signify italicized words by underlining them.

One of the uses of italic type is to set off the words that appear in certain kinds of names and titles. Most often, you have occasion to use italics for the titles of book- or pamphlet-length published materials. Besides being a convention, the use of italics for titles can also protect meaning in some instances. If you wrote "I don't really like Huckleberry Finn," a reader might be uncertain (unless the context gave a clue) whether you were revealing a dislike for Mark Twain's novel or for the character of that name in the novel. Simply by underlining (italicizing) the proper name, you could indicate unambiguously that you disliked the novel, not the character.

How do you decide whether a poem is long enough to have its title underlined? As with most relative matters, the extreme cases are easily determinable. Obviously, a sonnet would not qualify as a long poem, but Milton's *Paradise Lost* would. It is the middle-length poem that causes indecision. A reliable rule of thumb is this: if the poem was ever published as a separate book or if it could conceivably be published as a separate book, it can be considered long enough to have its title underlined. According to that guideline, T. S. Eliot's *The Wasteland* would be considered a long poem, but his "The Love Song of J. Alfred Prufrock" would be considered a short poem and therefore should be enclosed in quotation marks (see **84**). But if you cannot decide whether a poem is "long" or "short," either underline the title or enclose it in quotation marks and use that system consistently throughout the paper.

84 Titles, in Quotation Marks

The titles of articles, essays, short poems, songs, chapters of books, short stories, and episodes of radio and television programs should be enclosed in quotation marks.

Examples of titles that need to be enclosed with quotation marks:

84

1. Thomas Gray's Elegy Written in a Country Churchyard is reputed to be the most anthologized poem in the English language.

rewrite:

   Thomas Gray's "Elegy Written in a Country Churchyard" is reputed to be the most anthologized poem in the English language.

   (*quotation marks for the title of a short poem*)

2. Hollis Alpert's <u>Movies Are Better Than the Stage</u> first appeared in the <u>Saturday Review of Literature</u>.

rewrite:

   Hollis Alpert's "Movies Are Better Than the Stage" first appeared in the <u>Saturday Review of Literature</u>.

   (*quotation marks for the title of an article in a periodical*)

3. 'Raindrops Keep Falling on My Head' set exactly the right mood for the bicycle caper in <u>Butch Cassidy and the Sundance Kid</u>.

rewrite:

"Raindrops Keep Falling on My Head" set exactly the right mood for the bicycle caper in <u>Butch Cassidy and the Sundance Kid</u>.

(*quotation marks for the title of a song*)

4. On Tuesday evening, I saw The Homecoming, an unusually poignant episode of <u>M*A*S*H</u>.

rewrite:

On Tuesday evening, I saw "The Homecoming," an unusually poignant episode of <u>M*A*S*H</u>.

(*quotation marks for the title of an episode of a radio or television program*)

The general rule here is that the titles of material that is *part* of a book or a periodical or a program should be enclosed in quotation marks.

The title of a paper that you write should not be enclosed in quotation marks, nor should it be underlined. If your title contains elements that are normally underlined or enclosed in quotation marks, those elements, of course, should be underlined or enclosed in quotation marks.

The right and the wrong formats of a title for a paper submitted as a class assignment or for publication are illustrated here in typescript:

84

WRONG:

```
"The Evolution of Courtly Love in Medieval
Literature"
```

<u>The Evolution of Courtly Love in Medieval Literature</u>

RIGHT:

> The Evolution of Courtly Love in Medieval Literature

> The Evolution of Courtly Love in Chaucer's <u>Troilus</u> <u>and</u> <u>Criseyde</u>

> Courtly Love in Herrick's "Corinna's Going a-Maying" and Marvell's "To His Coy Mistress"

> The Shift in Meaning of the Word <u>Love</u> in Renaissance Lyrics

> "One Giant Step for Mankind"--Historic Words for a Historic Occasion

85   Italicize Words

Underline (italicize) words referred to as words.

Examples of words that should be underlined (italicized).

1. She questioned the appropriateness of the word honesty in this context.

rewrite:

> She questioned the appropriateness of the word <u>honesty</u> in this context.

2. My dictionary defines dudgeon as a "sullen, angry, or indignant humor."

rewrite:

> My dictionary defines <u>dudgeon</u> as a "sullen, angry, or indignant humor."

3. Unquestionably, trudged is a more specific verb than walked.

85

rewrite:

Unquestionably, <u>trudged</u> is a more specific verb than <u>walked</u>.

4. Look, for example, at his use of purely subjective words like marvelous, exquisite, and wondrous.

rewrite:

Look, for example, at his use of purely subjective words like <u>marvelous</u>, <u>exquisite</u>, and <u>wondrous</u>.

One of the uses of the graphic device of underlining (italics) is to distinguish a word being used as a *word* from that same word used as a symbol for a thing or an idea. Looking at two similar sentences can help us to see what difference in meaning is created by underlining or not underlining some word in the sentences:

She questioned the appropriateness of honesty in this context.

She questioned the appropriateness of <u>honesty</u> in this context.

85

Both of these sentences have the same words in the same order. The only difference between them is that in the second sentence, one of the words is underlined (italicized). That underlining of the word **honesty** makes for a difference in the meaning of the two sentences. The first sentence signifies that what is being challenged is the appropriateness of the thing (the abstract quality) designated by the word **honesty;** the second sentence signifies that what is being questioned is the appropriateness of the word only. Underlining (italicizing) the word **honesty** helps the reader to read the sentence as the writer intended it to be read—namely, that it was the word, not the virtue, that was being questioned.

An alternative but less common device for marking words used as words is to enclose the words in quotation marks, as in this example:

The heavy use of such sensory diction as "juicy," "empurpled," "smooth," "creaked," "murmuring" helps to evoke the scene and make it palpable to the reader.

Since both devices are authorized by convention, you should adopt one system and use it consistently. The use of italics is probably the safer of the two systems, however, because quotation marks are also used to enclose quoted words and phrases, as in the sentence

We heard her say "yes."

(Here *yes* is not being referred to as a word but is a quotation of what she said.)

86 Italicize Foreign Words

Underline (italicize) foreign words and phrases, unless they have become naturalized or Anglicized.

Examples of foreign words and phrases that should be underlined (italicized):

1. Why does the advertiser, whose mouthpiece is the copywriter, allow himself to be presented before the public as a poet malgré lui?

rewrite:

Why does the advertiser, whose mouthpiece is the copywriter, allow himself to be presented before the public as a poet <u>malgré lui</u>?

2. The advice to begin a short story as close to the climax as possible is a heritage of Horace's advice to begin a narrative in medias res rather than ab ovo.

rewrite:

The advice to begin a short story as close to the climax as possible is a heritage of Horace's advice to begin a narrative <u>in medias res</u> rather than <u>ab ovo</u>.

86

3. There had been a remarkable revival in the late 1960s of the Weltschmerz that characterized the poetry of the Romantics.

rewrite:

There had been a remarkable revival in the late 1960s of the <u>Weltschmerz</u> that characterized the poetry of the Romantics.

So that the reader will not be even momentarily mystified by the sudden intrusion of strange-looking words into a stream of English words, writers use italics to underscore foreign words and phrases. The graphic device of italics does not ensure, of course, that the reader will be able to translate the foreign expression, but it does prevent confusion by alerting the reader to the presence of non-English words.

Some foreign words and phrases, like habeas corpus, divorcée, mania, siesta, subpoena, have been used so often in an English context that they have been accepted into the vocabulary as "naturalized" or "Anglicized" words and therefore as not needing to be underlined (italicized). Since dictionaries have a system for indicating which foreign words and phrases have become naturalized and which have not, you should consult a dictionary when you are in doubt about the current status of a particular foreign word or phrase.

An exception to the rule is that proper nouns designating foreign persons, places, and institutions, even when they retain their native spelling and pronunciation, are *always* set forth without underlining (italics). None of the French proper nouns in the following sentence should be italicized (underlined): "Pierre Chardin thought that the Bibliothèque Nationale was on the Champs Élysées in Paris."

86

87   Hyphen, for Compound Words

Compound words should be hyphenated.

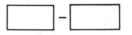

Examples of compound words that need to be hyphenated:

1. Because I had the normal six year old's "sweet tooth," I was irresistibly lured by the candy store.

rewrite:
Because I had the normal six-year-old's "sweet tooth," I was irresistibly lured by the candy store.

2. She was attracted to antiEstablishment movements because they lacked policy making administrators.

rewrite:
She was attracted to anti-Establishment movements because they lacked policy-making administrators.

3. They scheduled the examinations in three quarter hour segments.

rewrite:
They scheduled the examinations in three quarter-hour segments.

4. She preferred eighteenth century literature because of its urbanity.

rewrite:
She preferred eighteenth-century literature because of its urbanity.

5. A five or six story building should be all you will need for that kind of plant operation.

rewrite:
A five- or six-story building should be all you will need for that kind of plant operation.

87

6. Jim Paisley was the only new car dealer in town.
rewrite:
   Jim Paisley was the only new-car dealer in town.

English reveals its Germanic origins in its tendency to form compounds—that is, to take two or more words and join them to create a single unit that designates a thing or a concept quite different from what the individual words designate. A familiar example is the word *basketball*. When the two distinct words *basket* and *ball* were first joined to designate an athletic game or the kind of ball used in that game, the words were linked by a hyphen: *basket-ball*. When repeated use had made this new compound familiar to readers, the hyphen was dropped, and the two words were printed as a single word, with no break between the two constituent parts.

   Dozens of words in English have made this transition from a hyphenated compound to a single amalgamated word (e.g., *skyscraper*, *briefcase*, *airport*). But hundreds of compounds are still printed with a hyphen, either because they have not been used enough to achieve status as unmarked hybrids or because the absence of a hyphen would lead to ambiguity. A reliable dictionary will indicate which compounds have made the passage and which have not.

   With the exception of those words that have become recognized amalgams, a hyphen should be used to link

(a) two or more words functioning as a single grammatical unit.

> his **never-say-die** attitude (adjective)
> the junkyard had a huge **car-crusher** (noun)
> the hoodlums **pistol-whipped** him (verb)
> he conceded the point **willy-nilly** (adverb)

87

(b) two-word numbers (from 21 to 99) when they are written out.

twenty-one, thirty-six, forty-eight, ninety-nine

(c) combinations with prefixes **ex-** and **self-**.

ex-president, ex-wife, self-denial, self-contradictory

(d) combinations with prefixes like **anti-, pro-, pre-, post-,** when the second element in the combinations begins with a capital letter or a number.

anti-Establishment, pro-American, pre-1929, post-1945

(e) combinations with prefixes like **anti-, pro-, pre-, re-, semi-, sub-, over-,** when the second element begins with the letter that occurs at the end of the prefix.

anti-intellectual, pro-oxidant, pre-election, re-entry, semi-independent, sub-basement, over-refined

(f) combinations where the unhyphenated compound might be mistaken for another word.

re-cover (the chair)
recover (the lost wallet)
re-sign (the contract)
resign (the office)
co-op (a co-operative apartment)
coop (a pen for chickens)

87

With the exceptions noted in **(d)** and **(e)**, compounds formed with prefixes now tend to be written as a single word (for example, *antiknock, nonrestrictive, preconscious, subdivision, postgraduate*). From extensive reading, one develops a sense for those compounds that have been used often enough to become a single word in English.

Frequently in writing, only a hyphen will clarify ambiguous syntax. In sentence **3**, for instance, a reader would have difficulty determining whether the examination was divided into three segments of fifteen minutes each (a meaning that would be clearly signaled by this placement of the hyphen: **three quarter-hour segments**) or whether it was divided into segments of forty-five minutes duration (a meaning that is clearly signaled by this placement of hyphens: **three-quarter-hour segments**). There is a similar ambiguity in sentence **6**, **Jim Paisley was the only new car dealer in town**. A speaker would be able to clarify the ambiguous syntax of that sentence by the appropriate intonation of the voice. But in writing, only a hyphen will make clear whether the writer meant to say that Jim Paisley was the only new **car-dealer** in town or that he was the only **new-car** dealer in town.

In sentence **4**, the phrase **eighteenth century** is hyphenated because it is functioning as a compound adjective modifying the noun **literature**. But **eighteenth century** would not be a compound adjective and therefore would not be hyphenated if sentence **4** were phrased this way: **She preferred the literature of the eighteenth century** . . . .

Sentence **5** shows how to hyphenate when there is more than one term on the left side of the hyphenation (**five-, six-**). In this way, **story** need not be repeated (as in **A five-story or six-story building** . . .). In typing, insert a space after the hyphen if the hyphen is not immediately followed by the word it is meant to join (**five- or**; NOT: **five-or**).

87

88   Hyphen, to Divide Words

A word can be broken and hyphenated at the end of a line only at a syllable-break; a one-syllable word can never be broken and hyphenated.

Examples of words improperly syllabified:

1. bell-igerent   *rewrite:* bel-ligerent
2. stopp-ing   *rewrite:* stop-ping
3. rigo-rous   *rewrite:* rigor-ous
4. a-bout   *rewrite:* about
5. comm-unity   *rewrite:* commu-nity
6. wrench-ed   *rewrite:* wrenched

For the writer, two valuable bits of information are supplied by the initial entry of every word in the dictionary: (1) the spelling of the word, (2) the syllabification of the word. Words of more than two syllables can be broken and hyphenated at more than one place. The word **belligerent**, for instance, is entered this way in the dictionary: **bel·lig·er·ent**. If that word occurred at the end of a line and you saw that you could not get the whole word in the remaining space, you could break the word and hyphenate it at any of the syllables marked with a raised period. But you could not break the word in any of the following places: **bell·igerent**, **belli·gerent**, **bellige·rent**.

Since the syllabification of English words is often unpredictable, it is safest to consult a dictionary when you are in doubt about where syllable-breaks occur. But after a while, you learn certain "tricks" about syllabification that save you a trip to the dictionary. A word can usually be broken

(a) after a prefix (**con-**, **ad-**, **un-**, **im-**).
(b) before a suffix (**-tion**, **-ment**, **-less**, **-ous**, **-ing**).

88

(c) between double consonants (**oc-cur-rence**, **cop-per**, **stop-ping**, **prig-gish**).

One-syllable words, however, can never be divided and hyphenated, no matter how long they are. So if you come to the end of a line and find that you do not have enough space to squeeze in single-syllable words like **horde**, **grieve**, **stopped**, **quaint**, **strength**, **wrenched**, leave the space blank and write the whole word on the next line. You have no choice.

Even in the interest of preserving a right-hand margin, you should not divide a word so that only one or two letters of it stand at the end of the line or at the beginning of the next line. Faced with divisions like **a-bout**, **o-cean**, **un-healthy**, **grass-y**, **dioram-a**, **flor-id**, **smok-er**, **live-ly**, you should put the whole word on that line or on the next line. Remember that the hyphen itself takes up one space.

89 Numbers

89

Observe the conventions governing the use of numbers in written copy.

Examples of violations of the conventions:

1. 522 men reported to the recruiting center.

rewrite:

> **Five hundred twenty-two** men reported to the recruiting center.

> **or**

> A total of **522** men reported to the recruiting center.

2. During the first half of the 20th century, 28 4-year colleges and 14 2-year colleges adopted collective bargaining.

rewrite:
> During the first half of the **twentieth** century, **twenty-eight four**-year colleges and **fourteen two**-year colleges adopted collective bargaining.

3. The cocktail party started at four P.M. in the afternoon.

rewrite:
> The cocktail party started at **4:00** P.M.
>
> **or**
>
> The cocktail party started at **four o'clock in the afternoon**.

4. An account of the Wall Street crash of October twenty-ninth, nineteen hundred and twenty-nine, begins on page fifty-five.

rewrite:
> An account of the Wall Street crash of October **29**, **1929**, begins on page **55**.

5. About six and a half % of the stores were selling a gross of three-by-five index cards for more than thirty-six dollars and thirty-eight cents.

rewrite:
> About **6½ percent** of the stores were selling a gross of **3″ × 5″** index cards for more than **$36.38**.

The most common conventions governing the use of numbers in written copy are as follows:

89

(a) Do not begin a sentence with an arabic numeral; spell out the number or recast the sentence (see sentence **1**).

(b) Spell out any number of less than three digits (or any number under 101) when the number is used as an adjective modifying a noun (see sentence **2**).

(c) Always use arabic numerals with **a.m.** and **p.m.** (or **A.M.** and **P.M.**) and do not add the redundant **o'clock** and **morning** or **afternoon** (see sentence **3**).

(d) Use arabic numerals for dates and page numbers (see sentence **4**).

(e) Use arabic numerals for addresses (618 N. 29th St.), dollars and cents ($4.68, $0.15 or 15 cents), decimals (3.14, 0.475), degrees (52° F, 26° C), measurements (especially when abbreviations are used: 3″ × 5″, 3.75 mi., 2 ft. 9 in., 6′2″ tall, but *six feet tall*), percentages (6% or 6 percent, but always use **percent** with fractional percentages—6½ percent or 6.5 percent) (see sentence 5).

90   Capitalization

Observe the conventions governing the capitalization of certain words.

Examples of words that need to be capitalized:

1. President Ronald Reagan informed the members of congress that he was appointing ms. Margaret Heckler as the united states ambassador to Ireland.

rewrite:

President Ronald Reagan informed the members of Congress that he was appointing Ms. Margaret Heckler as the United States ambassador to Ireland.

2. The title of the article in the *New Yorker* was "The time of illusion."

rewrite:

The title of the article in the *New Yorker* was "The Time of Illusion."

3. Dr. Thomas J. Cade, a professor in the division of biological sciences at Cornell university, has been supervising the breeding of peregrines captured in the arctic, the west, and the pacific northwest.

rewrite:

Dr. Thomas J. Cade, a professor in the Division of Biological Sciences at Cornell University, has been supervising the breed-

90

ing of peregrines captured in the Arctic, the West, and the Pacific Northwest.

4. The prime vacation time for most Americans is the period between the fourth of July and labor day.

rewrite:

The prime vacation time for most Americans is the period between the Fourth of July and Labor Day.

5. The korean troops resisted the incursion of the communist forces.

rewrite:

The Korean troops resisted the incursion of the Communist forces.

In general, the convention governing capitalization is that the first letter of the proper name (that is, the particular or exclusive name) of persons, places, things, institutions, agencies, and such should be capitalized. While the tendency today is to use lower-case letters for many words that formerly were written or printed with capital letters (for instance, *biblical reference* instead of ***B**iblical reference*), the use of capital letters still prevails in the following cases:

(a) The first letter of the first word of a sentence.

They were uncertain about which words should be capitalized.

90

(b) The first letter of the first word of every line of traditional English verse.

Little fly,
Thy summer's play
My thoughtless hand
Has brushed away.

(c) All nouns, pronouns, verbs, adjectives, adverbs, and first and last words of titles of publications and other artistic works.

Remembrance of Things Past (see **83**)

"**The P**lace of the **E**nthymeme in **R**hetorical **T**heory" (see **84**)

"**A T**ent **T**hat **F**amilies **C**an **L**ive **I**n"

The Return of the Pink Panther

(d) The first name, middle name or initial, and last name of a person, real or fictional.

T. S. Eliot	**S**ylvia **M**arie **M**ikkelsen
David **C**opperfield	**A**chilles

(e) The names and abbreviations of villages, towns, cities, counties, states, nations, and regions.

Chillicothe, **O**hio	**F**ranklin **C**ounty
U.S.A.	**S**oviet **U**nion
Indochina	**A**rctic **C**ircle
the **W**estern world	**S**outh **A**merica
the **M**idwestern states	the **S**outh (but: we drove south)

(f) The names of rivers, lakes, falls, oceans, mountains, deserts, parks.

the **M**ississippi **R**iver	**A**tlantic
the **G**rand **T**etons	**Y**ellowstone **N**ational **P**ark
Lake **E**rie	**V**ictoria **F**alls

90

(g) The names and abbreviations of businesses, industries, institutions, agencies, schools, political parties, religious denominations, and philosophical, literary, and artistic movements.

University of **N**ebraska	**D**emocrats
the **R**epublican convention	**C.I.A.**
Dow **C**hemical **C**orporation	**S**cott, **F**oresman and **C**ompany
Communist(s) (but: a communist ideology)	**S**mithsonian **I**nstitution

Victorian literature
Thomistic philosophy

Japan Air Lines
the Pentagon
Pure Land Buddhism

(h) The titles of historical events, epochs, and periods.

Renaissance
World War II
the Middle Ages
Reformation

Thirty Years' War
Ice Age
the Battle of Gettysburg
the Depression

(i) Honorary and official titles when they precede the name of the person.

Rabbi Balfour Brickner
the Duke of Cornwall
Pope John Paul II
His (Her) Excellency

Bishop Tsuji
General Patton
Chief Justice Burger
Queen Elizabeth

(j) The names of weekdays, months, holidays, holy days, and other special days or periods.

Christmas Eve
Passover
Lent
Mardi Gras

Memorial Day
the Fourth of July
National Book Week
the first Sunday in June

90

(k) The names and abbreviations of the books and divisions of the Bible and other sacred books (no italics for these titles).

Genesis
Matt. (Gospel of Matthew)
Epistle to the Romans
King James Version
Talmud
Book of Job
Pss. (Psalms)

Pentateuch
Acts of the Apostles
Koran
Scriptures
Bhagavad Gita
Lotus Sutra
Science and Health

Exceptions: Do *not* capitalize words like the underlined in the following examples:

the African <u>coast</u> (but: the West Coast)

the <u>river</u> Elbe (but: the Elbe River)

<u>northern</u> Wisconsin

the <u>federal government</u>

the <u>senator</u> from Wyoming

the <u>presidential</u> itinerary

the <u>municipal library</u>

the <u>county courthouse</u>

in the <u>autumn</u>

they headed <u>west</u>

NEVER-SAY NEVERISMS

William Safire

(If you have absorbed the lessons of this handbook, you will be able to detect what is wrong in each of the following proscriptions, which William Safire calls "never-say neverisms."*)

1. Remember to never split an infinitive.
2. The passive voice should never be used.
3. Avoid run-on sentences they are hard to read.
4. Don't use no double negatives.
5. Use the semicolon properly, always use it where it is appropriate; and never where it isn't.
6. Reserve the apostrophe for it's proper use and omit it when its not needed.
7. Do not put statements in the negative form.
8. Verbs has to agree with their subjects.
9. No sentence fragments.

*From William Safire, "The Fumblerules of Grammar," *The New York Times Magazine,* November 4, 1979 p. 16, and "Fumblerule Follow-Up," November 25, 1979, p. 14. Copyright © 1979 by The New York Times Company. Reprinted by permission.

10. Proofread carefully to see if you any words out.

11. Avoid commas, that are not necessary.

12. If you reread your work, you will find on rereading that a great deal of repetition can be avoided by rereading and editing.

13. A writer must not shift your point of view.

14. Eschew dialect, irregardless.

15. And don't start a sentence with a conjunction.

16. Don't overuse exclamation marks!!!

17. Place pronouns as close as possible, especially in long sentences, as of ten or more words, to their antecedents.

18. Hyphenate between syllables and avoid un-necessary hyphens.

19. Write all adverbial forms correct.

20. Don't use contractions in formal writing.

21. Writing carefully, dangling participles must be avoided.

22. It is incumbent on us to avoid archaisms.

23. If any word is improper at the end of a sentence, a linking verb is.

24. Steer clear of incorrect forms of verbs that have snuck in the language.

25. Take the bull by the hand and avoid mixed metaphors.

26. Avoid trendy locutions that sound flaky.

27. Never, ever use repetitive redundancies.

28. Everyone should be careful to use a singular pronoun with singular nouns in their writing.

29. If I've told you once, I've told you a thousand times, resist hyperbole.

30. Also, avoid awkward or affected alliteration.

31. Don't string too many prepositional phrases together unless you are walking through the valley of the shadow of death.

32. Never use a long word when a diminutive one will do.

33. If a dependent clause precedes an independent clause put a comma after the dependent clause.

34. One will not have needed the future perfect in one's entire life.

35. Unqualified superlatives are the worst of all.

36. If this were subjunctive, I'm in the wrong mood.

37. Always pick on the correct idiom.

38. "Avoid overuse of 'quotation "marks." ' "

39. The adverb always follows the verb.

40. Last but not least, avoid clichés like the plague; seek viable alternatives.

41. Surly grammarians insist that all words ending in "ly" are adverbs.

42. De-accession euphemisms.

43. In statements involving two word phrases, make an all out effort to use hyphens.

44. It is not resultful to transform one part of speech into another by prefixing, suffixing, or other alterings.

45. Avoid colloquial stuff.

FORMAT OF THE RESEARCH PAPER

GENERAL INSTRUCTIONS

A research paper reports the results of some investigation, experiment, interview, or reading that you have done. Some of the ordinary papers you write are also based on personal investigations, interviews, and reading, and when your paper is based on data derived from research, you should acknowledge the source of the data. For instance, you can reveal the source of information or quotations by saying, right in the text of your paper, "Mr. Stanley Smith, the director of the Upward Bound project, with whom I talked last week, confirmed the rumor that . . . ." or "James Reston said in his column in last Sunday's *New York Times* that . . . ." Authors of research papers also use identifying lead-ins like those, but in addition, they supply—usually in parenthetical references—any further information (such as the exact date of the newspaper they are quoting from and the number of the page from which the quotation was taken) that readers would need if they wanted to check the sources. By revealing this specific information about the source, authors enable readers to check the accuracy and fairness of the reporting, and they enhance their credibility with readers.

In the pages that follow, we will present some advice about gathering and reporting material from outside sources, some models of parenthetical forms, and a sample research paper. The instructor or the publication that you write for may prescribe a format that differs from the advice given here, but if no specific instructions are given, you can follow these suggestions and models with the assurance that they conform to the prevailing conventions for research papers written in most fields. The format for documenting references, citations, and quotations may differ slightly from discipline to discipline, but whether you are writing a research paper in the humanities or in the physical sciences, the same kind of basic information about the sources is supplied in the documentation.

A   Selecting an Appropriate Subject

Taking special care in selecting an appropriate subject for your research paper will, in the long run, make the task of writing the paper easier and increase your chances of getting a good grade for your efforts. Sometimes you will have a completely free choice of a subject for your paper; at other times your instructor will set up a list of subjects or a general category of subjects from which you must choose. In either case, the ultimate choice of a specific subject will be yours. Make this choice conscientiously and judiciously.

A number of considerations will guide you in selecting an appropriate subject: (1) the physical limits set for the paper, either in terms of the number of words (e.g., 2500–3000 words) or in terms of the number of pages (e.g., 8–10 pages); (2) the time available to you, from the initial assignment to the final due date; (3) your particular interests; (4) the research facilities available to you; (5) the defined limits of the subject; and (6) a determination of the main point you want to make about the subject you choose.

Suppose that from a list of topics suggested by your instructor, you chose this one: The Use of Computers in the Schools. You chose that subject partly because it interests you (3) and partly because you are sure that your school library contains lots of material on this timely subject (4). Because you have only five weeks in which to do the research and write the paper (2) and because the instructor set a limit of 2000–2500 words (8–10 double-spaced pages at 250 words per page) for the paper (1), you realize that you must narrow the broad subject that you have chosen (5) and determine the main point you want to make about the narrowed subject that you finally select (6).

By chipping away at your broad subject, you can get it down to manageable proportions. You decide that you do not want to consider all the possible uses of computers in the schools, so you confine yourself to word-processors. *Schools* is too broad a category for this paper, so you decide to concentrate on the undergraduate college scene. You further narrow the subject by specifying the use of the word-processor in the college freshman composition classroom. Now that you have a sharply defined subject (5) that can be managed within the limits set for you (1, 2, 3, 4), you must decide what point you want to make about that subject (6). After careful deliberation, you settle on a focus and decide to formulate that focus in a statement of purpose rather than in a thesis sentence: I want to investigate some of the successes that colleges in the United States have had in improving the writing of students by using word-processors in freshman composition courses.

A

Now you are ready to go to the library to find some usable material on that sharply defined topic.

B Using the Library

Unless your research paper is simply a report of a lab experiment, a questionnaire, or a series of interviews that you conducted, it will depend largely on your reading of books and articles. The main source of books and articles is the library—either the public library or the college library. Perhaps the chief benefit that you derive from doing a research paper is that this exercise forces you to become acquainted with the library and its resources. Becoming aware of the wealth of knowledge stored in the library and getting to know *where* the various pockets of wealth are located in the library and *how* to use them will be a valuable part of your general education.

The best way to get acquainted with the library is to visit it, to look around, to examine the card catalogue, to take some books down off the shelves and open them, and, above all, to *use the library*. But if you want to speed up the getting-acquainted process, you can consult a book like Eugene P. Sheehy's *A Guide to Reference Books*, which you can find on the reference shelves of the library. (The 9th edition was published in 1980—the 10th edition should be available in 1987. It is published by the American Library Association: Chicago.) What follows is an introduction to a few general reference sources and some bibliographical sources, which would be both generally helpful in your pursuit of knowledge and particularly helpful to you in preparing to write a research paper.

B

GENERAL REFERENCE SOURCES

Encyclopedias

Multivolume encyclopedias are the most familiar and usually the most available source of information on a wide range of subjects. The treatment of topics in an encyclopedia varies in length from a few sentences to several pages, though many of the entries, especially the longer ones, list pertinent books and articles that you can consult for further information.

The encyclopedia is a good starting point for a research project, but ordinarily it should not be the stopping point. You will have to go on to more specialized reference sources. Here are three well-known multivolume encyclopedias and one very useful single-volume encyclopedia. All of them cover a wide range of subjects, are international in their scope, and cover all centuries, but each one is strong in a particular area. The first two publish yearbooks, which cover the main events and topics of the previous year.

Encyclopedia Americana. Danbury, CT: Grolier Educational Corp., 1980. 30 volumes. Particularly useful for anything connected with the United States.

Encyclopaedia Britannica. Chicago: Encyclopaedia Britannica Educational Corp., 1984. 30 volumes. Strong on both American and British topics.

Chambers's Encyclopedia. Elmsford, NY: Maxwell Scientific International, 1973. 15 volumes. Particularly strong on British topics.

The New Columbia Encyclopedia. 4th ed. New York: Columbia University Press, 1975. One volume. More than 50,000 articles on the humanities, social sciences, life and physical sciences, and geography packed into 3,052 pages.

B

Almanacs and Other General Sources of Facts and Statistics

Almanacs are a rich storehouse of factual and statistical information. They always retain the basic historical, geographical, social, political, and statistical information, but each year they add the pertinent factual and statistical information for the previous year. Here are the titles of two inexpensive paperback almanacs and the titles of two other sources of facts and statistics that can be found in the reference room of the library:

Information Please Almanac. New York: Simon and Schuster, 1947– Published annually.

World Almanac. New York: Newspaper Enterprise Association, Inc., 1868–   . Published annually.

Facts on File. New York: Facts on File, Inc., 1940–   . Published weekly. A valuable source of information about the important events of the week.

U.S. Bureau of the Census: Statistical Abstract of the United States. Washington, D.C.: Government Printing Office, 1879–   . Published annually. The most comprehensive source of statistical information about all aspects of American life.

Handbooks

B

Another source of general information about a particular field is the one-volume reference work that we will label *handbook.* Handbooks contain some of the same kinds of information supplied by multivolume encyclopedias, but the entries are shorter, and they are restricted to a special field, like literature or business. But precisely because they are restricted to a particular field, they often cover topics that are considered too minor or specialized for inclusion in a multivolume encyclopedia. In a handbook, you can expect to find these kinds of information about the field covered: definitions of key terms and concepts; identifications of allusions; accounts of historical or ideological movements; short biographical sketches; summaries of important books; bibliographies. Here is a list of a few important handbooks, one for each of seven different fields.

The Reader's Encyclopedia. Ed. William R. Benet. 2nd ed. New York: Crowell, 1965. A handbook of world literature.

Oxford Companion to the Theatre. Ed. Phyllis Hartnoll. 3rd ed. New York: Oxford University Press, 1983. A handy reference source for information about world drama, from its beginnings in ancient Greece.

Oxford Companion to Film. Ed. Liz-Anne Bawden. New York: Oxford University Press, 1976. One of the many "Oxford Companions," about an art form that has become a prominent part of everyday life.

Encyclopedia of Banking and Finance. Ed. Ferdinand L. Garcia. 8th ed. Boston: The Bankers Publishing Co., 1983. An invaluable one-volume reference work for anything connected with business.

The Concise Encyclopedia of Western Philosophy and Philosophers. Ed. J. O. Urmson. New York: Hawthorn Books, 1960. Brief but authoritative information about philosophy and philosophers.

Dictionary of Education. Ed. Carter V. Good. 3rd ed. New York: McGraw-Hill, 1973. More than a dictionary, this reference work supplies the usual kind of handbook information about the field of professional education.

International Cyclopedia of Music and Musicians. Ed. Bruce Bohle. 10th ed. New York: Dodd, Mead, 1975. One of a number of very good one-volume handbooks on music.

B

Biographical Dictionaries
Encyclopedias and handbooks will provide you with brief biographical sketches of prominent men and women. But for fuller accounts of persons, both living and de-

ceased, and for biographical sketches of less prominent people, you will have to go to the more specialized biographical dictionaries. Listed below are five of the best-known and most useful of these specialized biographical dictionaries.

Dictionary of National Biography (sometimes referred to as the *DNB*). New York: Oxford University Press, 1921. 22 volumes (a reissue of the original 66-volume set published in 1885). Lives of about 18,000 *deceased* subjects of Great Britain and Commonwealth dependencies. Supplements bring the coverage up to 1970.

Who's Who. London: A & C Black, Ltd., 1849– . Published annually. Biographical information about distinguished *living* men and women of Great Britain.

Dictionary of American Biography (sometimes referred to as the *DAB*). New York: Scribner's, 1927–1981. 17 volumes. The equivalent of the British *DNB*, this multivolume set gives the biographies of prominent and not-so-prominent *deceased* Americans.

Who's Who in America. Chicago: Marquis, 1899– . Published every second year. The equivalent of the British *Who's Who*, this reference source provides biographical information about notable *living* Americans.

International Who's Who. London: Europa Publications, 1935– . Published annually. Information about the lives of prominent *living* men and women of all nations.

B

SPECIALIZED BIBLIOGRAPHIES

The reference works mentioned in the previous sections can give you general information that could be useful for your personal enlightenment or for your classwork. But since a research paper is usually written about a narrow topic in a specialized field, you will need more specific information than those general reference works can provide. You must track down books, articles, pamphlets, and monographs that deal more particularly with the topic of your paper. To track down that more specific material, you can turn to *bibliographical reference works*—works that list the authors or editors, titles, and publication information of published books, articles, and reviews on a particular topic. Fortunately, there are a number of general and specialized bibliographical guides.

A helpful guide to available bibliographies is the *Bibliographic Index* (New York: H. W. Wilson, 1937–   ). This guide to the bibliographies that have been published in books, pamphlets, bulletins, and periodicals is arranged alphabetically according to subject. If you were doing a research paper on the trucking industry, for example, and wanted to find out whether any bibliographies on this subject had been published, you could consult several volumes of the *Bibliographic Index* under the main subject-heading of *Transportation*. If you found a bibliography listed there on the trucking industry, you would then have to check the card catalogue to find out whether your library had that bibliography. Once you got your hands on that bibliography, you would find an extensive list of books and articles dealing with the trucking industry. Then you would once again have to consult the card catalogue to see whether your library had any of the books and articles listed in that bibliography.

B

PERIODICAL INDEXES

Of more practical use, perhaps, to the undergraduate or informal researcher are the general and specialized indexes to reviews and articles in popular magazines and newspapers and in various scholarly journals.

General Periodical Indexes

Book Review Digest. 1905–   . Summarizes reviews of books from a large number of periodicals. Gives critical reception of books reviewed.

Nineteenth Century Reader's Guide. 1890–1899. Periodicals for the last ten years of the 1800s.

Readers' Guide to Periodical Literature. 1900–   . An excellent guide for general purpose reading. Lists articles from a broad range of periodicals. Entries are by author, subject, and cross-listing. Most articles written for general public.

Specialized Periodical Indexes

Art Index. 1929–   .

Biological and Agricultural Index. 1964–   . Supersedes *Agricultural Index,* 1916–1964.

Business Periodicals Index. 1958–   . Supersedes *Industrial Arts Index,* 1913–1957.

Education Index. 1929–   .

General Science Index. 1978–   .

Humanities Index. 1974–   . Formerly *International Index,* 1907–1965, and *Social Sciences and Humanities Index,* 1965–1974.

Music Index. 1949–   .

Public Affairs Information Service Bulletin. 1915–   .

Social Sciences Index. 1974–   . Formerly *International Index,* 1907–1965 and *Social Sciences and Humanities Index,* 1965–1974.

United States Government Publications, Monthly Catalog. 1895–   .

B

MICROFORMS AND DATABASES

Besides the printed indexes to periodical literature, there are indexes recorded in such miniaturized forms as microfilms and microfiches and in on-line computerized databases. Whereas the printed indexes lag behind the current date anywhere from three months to a whole year, the indexes recorded in some of the electronic media can be frequently and easily updated so that they lag behind the current date by as little as a month. So if you need to compile a list of articles on a current topic, the indexes in microforms and databases may be your only resource.

The two microfilm indexes to periodical literature that you are most likely to find in your college or public library are the *Magazine Index* (Belmont, CA: Information Access Corporation) and the *National Newspaper Index* (Belmont, CA: Information Access Corporation). *Magazine Index*, which covers the most recent four years, indexes more than 400 magazines published in North America. In this alphabetical index, items are listed by subject, by title, by product names, by the names of people in the news, and by authors. Under each of those categories, the most recent articles are listed first. The *National Newspaper Index*, a similar index for national newspapers, indexes the most recent five years of the *New York Times*, *Wall Street Journal*, *Christian Science Monitor*, *Washington Post*, and *Los Angeles Times*. The microfilms for both these indexes are already loaded into two separate microfilm-readers that sit side by side on a table in the library, and all you have to do is turn on the machine and press the fast-wind or the slow-wind button to get to that part of the alphabetical listing that has what you are interested in.

B

Two of the computerized databases that you may find on-line in your local library are *Newsearch* (Belmont, CA: Information Access Corporation) and *Nexis* (Dayton, OH: Mead Data Central). The first of these, for instance, indexes some 400 magazines, 300 trade journals, 5 national newspapers, 700 law journals, and 700 business and management journals. To gain access to this vast reservoir of reference material, you may have to pay a fee, ranging from a few dollars to hundreds of dollars, depending on the number of minutes the search takes and the number of items printed out on the hard copy you are given. At present, this expensive resource is used mainly by graduate students, faculty, and funded researchers, but in order to gather a bibliography in a hurry on certain subjects, you might find it worth the cost to resort to this electronic reference tool. But in order to save yourself a lot of money, you would do well to seek the help of a librarian in the reference department.

ABSTRACTS

After compiling your list of potentially useful books and articles, you might be able to save yourself some wasted motions by consulting the appropriate *collection of abstracts*. By reading a 150–200-word abstract of any of the books and articles on your list, you should be able to tell whether that book or article contains information pertinent to your paper. Most of the scholarly fields now publish annual collections of abstracts of books and articles published during the previous year. The sciences have been publishing abstracts for a number of years, and recently the humanities have begun to publish annual abstracts. You can also use the collection of abstracts as a bibliographical source, since every abstract is headed with the name of the author, the title, and the publication information of the text being summarized.

THE CARD CATALOGUE

The card catalogue—the rows of file-drawers or, increasingly, the terminals which can call up their computerized equivalents—is a valuable resource. Not only does it indicate whether the library has the particular book or periodical you are seeking and where in the library stacks the book or periodical can be found, but it is also another resource for compiling a bibliography for a research project. A library usually has at least three cards in the files for a single book—an *author* card (usually called the "main entry" card), a *title* card, and one or more *subject* cards. **It is the subject cards that give you the best leads on books pertinent to your research project.** Under the appropriate subject heading will be grouped all the books that the library has on a particular subject. You can discover the "appropriate subject heading" from looking at the Library of Congress card for a book that you *know* is pertinent to your study, because on every Library of Congress card, one or more subject headings are suggested for a book.

Most libraries buy the printed cards prepared by a staff of classification experts at the Library of Congress in Washington, D.C. The Library of Congress (abbreviated L.C.) cards carry a lot of information. On page 172, three Library of Congress cards are displayed for a particular book, and the various parts of the card are tagged with letters of the alphabet. The interpretation of those various lettered parts is found on page 173.

B

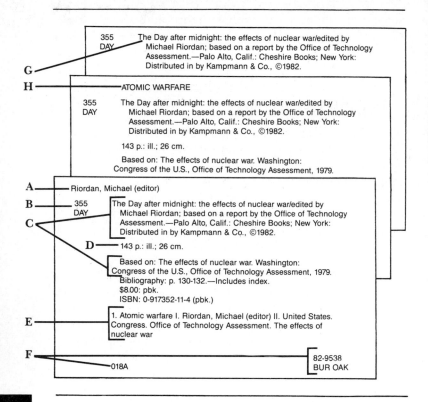

G — 355
      DAY   The Day after midnight: the effects of nuclear war/edited by
               Michael Riordan; based on a report by the Office of Technology
               Assessment.—Palo Alto, Calif.: Cheshire Books; New York:
               Distributed in by Kampmann & Co., ©1982.

H — ————————ATOMIC WARFARE

     355   The Day after midnight: the effects of nuclear war/edited by
     DAY   Michael Riordan; based on a report by the Office of Technology
               Assessment.—Palo Alto, Calif.: Cheshire Books; New York:
               Distributed in by Kampmann & Co., ©1982.

               143 p.: ill.; 26 cm.

               Based on: The effects of nuclear war. Washington:
               Congress of the U.S., Office of Technology Assessment, 1979.

A — Riordan, Michael (editor)
B — 355   The Day after midnight: the effects of nuclear war/edited by
     DAY   Michael Riordan; based on a report by the Office of Technology
C —   Assessment.—Palo Alto, Calif.: Cheshire Books; New York:
               Distributed in by Kampmann & Co., ©1982.

     D — 143 p.: ill.; 26 cm.

               Based on: The effects of nuclear war. Washington:
               Congress of the U.S., Office of Technology Assessment, 1979.
               Bibliography: p. 130-132.—Includes index.
               $8.00: pbk.
               ISBN: 0-917352-11-4 (pbk.)

E — 1. Atomic warfare I. Riordan, Michael (editor) II. United States.
     Congress. Office of Technology Assessment. The effects of
     nuclear war

F —   82-9538
      018A   BUR OAK

B

When you are compiling a bibliography for your research project, **the most important information for you to copy down from the L.C. card is the author**, **title**, **publication information**, **and call number of the book**. Of that information, the item most crucial for your gaining access to the book is the **call number**. That call number helps either you or the librarian to find the exact spot on the shelf where the book is stored.

A. The **name of the author** (last name first). This *author* card or *main entry card* will be found in the card catalogue in one of the drawers for the letter R.

B. The **call number of the book**, typed in by the library staff. This is the number you must copy down if you want to find the book yourself in the stacks or if you want one of the library clerks to get the book for you.

C. The **title of the book and publication information** about the book (i.e., the book is based on a study done for Congress by the U.S. Office of Technology Assessment in 1979).

D. This entry supplies information about the **physical makeup of the book**: there are 143 pages; there are illustrations; and the book is 26 centimeters in height.

E. This entry suggests **other headings** under which the book can be filed.

F. Technical information supplied for the use of the library staff.

G. The **title of the book**. If you knew the title of the book but didn't know the author, you could find the book by looking for this title card in the card catalogue.

H. A **subject heading for the book**, typed in block capitals by the library staff. Notice in E after the number 1 that *Atomic Warfare* is the first subject heading suggested by the Library of Congress Staff.

B

You should also be aware of another service that the card catalogue and the computer-accessing system can provide. Most of the time when you are faced with the task of writing a research paper, you do not know the authors and the titles of pertinent books. You can discover pertinent books by consulting the card catalogue or the computer under a subject heading that covers the topic of your research. But the key to discovering a list of books that would be useful for your research is getting the right subject heading. Looking for books under the wrong subject heading might yield the wrong kinds of books or no books at all.

The most helpful reference guide for finding the right subject heading is the two-volume *Library of Congress Subject Headings*, copies of which are readily available in almost every university or public library. Say that you were assigned to do a research paper on the history of parochial schools in the United States and wanted to find what books the university library had on the subject. Before consulting the card catalogue or the computer under the heading of "parochial schools," you would be well advised to look for that heading in one of the alphabetically arranged volumes of *Library of Congress Subject Headings*. There you would discover that "parochial schools" is not one of the recommended headings but that the recommended heading for the library's holdings on the topic is "church schools." Also under this heading in the book, you would find some *See also* references to related subjects, like "church and education," "private schools," and "religious education." By consulting the card catalogue or the computer under one of those headings, you would get a list of all the books in that library on the subject of church-related schools.

C Compiling a Bibliography

In compiling a bibliography—that is, your selected list of the relevant books and articles that you discovered by consulting the appropriate reference sources in the library—you should make a separate 3″ × 5″ card for each item. Each of these cards should contain the following information (see the sample cards on p. 176): (1) the call number of

the book or of the bound periodical in which you found the
article; (2) the name of the author or editor; (3) the title of
the book or article (and, in the case of the article, the title of
the magazine or journal in which the article was published);
(4) the publication information for the book (the place of
publication, the name of the publisher, and the publication
date) or the publication information for the article (the volume number of the magazine or journal in which the article
appeared, the date of the issue of that magazine or journal,
and the first and last page number of the article—e.g.,
341–358); (5) some kind of notation—e.g., a subject heading or an explanatory sentence—that will help you later on
in quickly identifying the particular area of your study
where this book or article fits in.

In filling out these bibliography cards, you should observe this guiding principle: the information recorded on
this card should be so complete and accurate that you
would never have to go back to the book or the periodical to
get or to check any information about it.

If you have been conscientious about gathering pertinent material for your research, you will have a much longer list of books and articles that you need or than you can
handle. You will have to trim your list to manageable proportions. That trimming will involve you in some kind of
evaluation of the available sources. Here are some criteria
that will help you select the most useful and reliable
sources: **(1)** the *date* of the book or article (for many studies,
usually the later the date of the source, the more useful or
reliable the information will be); **(2)** the *reputation* of the
author (if you cannot yourself judge the relative authorita-
tiveness of the author, you can consult biographical reference works or reviews of the book or citation indexes);
(3) the *status* of the publisher or of the periodical (in every
field of study, you soon develop a sense for those publishers and periodicals that have acquired a reputation for pub-

C

lishing thorough and reliable scholarship); **(4)** the degree of *pertinence* to your study (even a cursory examination of the available books and articles will often reveal that some of them are more relevant for your purposes than others are).

Here are two sample bibliography cards:

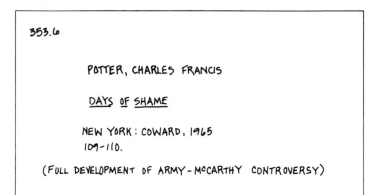

```
353.6

        POTTER, CHARLES FRANCIS

        DAYS OF SHAME

        NEW YORK: COWARD, 1965
        109-110.

    (FULL DEVELOPMENT OF ARMY-M°CARTHY CONTROVERSY)
```

```
070.92

      WHITE, THEODORE H.

IN  SEARCH  OF HISTORY: A PERSONAL ADVENTURE
        NEW YORK: HARPER, 1978
        395-396.


(LONG-TERM RESULTS OF                    ISBN NO.
  M°CARTHY ATTACK ON                     0-06-014599-4
 FOREIGN SERVICE OFFICERS)
```

In each instance the works were written ten to twenty years after the event—long enough to provide some historical perspective **(1)**. Each author carries a measure of authority (Potter was a U.S. Senator in the 1950s and Theodore White is a recognized journalist and historian) **(2)**. Both Coward McCann and Harper & Row are old, reputable publishing houses **(3)**. Pertinence to your study **(4)** then will help you to evaluate these two sources. If your subject is "McCarthyism" and you want to limit your discussion to its *immediate* impact on the military, the Potter book will likely be the better source. If, on the other hand, you want to examine the *long-term* results of the McCarthy era, particularly as it affected military and foreign policy, the White book will better suit your needs.

D   Notes

GATHERING NOTES

If you do enough research, you will eventually develop a system of gathering notes that works best for you. Some people, for instance, just scribble their notes on full sheets of paper or in spiral notebooks. Others record their notes and quotations on 3″ × 5″ or 4″ × 6″ cards—*one* note or quotation to a card. The advantage of recording notes on separate cards is that later you can select and arrange the cards to suit the order in which you are going to use them in your paper. It is considerably more difficult to select and arrange notes if they are written out, one after the other, on full sheets of paper. You could, of course, cut out notes from the full sheets, but that activity involves an extra step.

D

Each notecard should be self-contained—that is, it should contain all the information you would need to document that material properly if you used it in your paper. A notecard is self-contained if you never have to go back to the original source to recover any bit of information about the note. So each notecard should include the following:

1. The particular information you wish to record.

2. Your own shorthand system of referring to the source of the information—for example, the author's last name or a short version of the title—and the page(s) on which the information appears.

3. An indication of whether the note is a summary, a paraphrase, or a direct quotation.

(See the sample notecard on p. 181.)

ACCURACY IN NOTES

Whenever you are transmitting information that you have appropriated from others, you must be scrupulously careful about the accuracy of that information. The question of accuracy is complicated by considerations of whether the material you are transmitting represents a *summary* or a *paraphrase* or a *direct quotation*. If you are transmitting the material in the form of a direct quotation, that quotation must be reproduced exactly as it appeared in the original source. You must not inadvertently add or omit or misspell any words. If you deliberately add words to a direct quotation, you must put those words in square brackets:

> The President said, "He [William Bennet] significantly changed the direction in which the NEH [National Endowment for the Humanities] was headed that year [1985]."

If you deliberately omit words from a direct quotation, you must use ellipsis periods to signal the omission:

The authors of the report say, "Blending may seem simple to an adult who already knows how to read, but . . . it is a difficult step for many children."

If a word was misspelled in the original source, you must reproduce that misspelling in the quotation and signal that the misspelling is not yours by putting *sic* (thus) in square brackets:

"That is the most flattering complement [*sic*] I have ever received," Professor James said in a letter to the editor.

(See the *Ellipsis Periods* and *Square Brackets* on pp. 186–187.)

Accuracy is a more relative matter when you transmit appropriated information in the form of a paraphrase or a summary. What paraphrase and summary have in common is that they represent someone's attempt to render in one's own words information gathered from some outside source. The difference between a paraphrase and a summary is that a paraphrase tends to be a translation of something said in a few sentences, whereas a summary tends to be a translation of something said over several paragraphs or pages. We can objectively judge the accuracy of a direct quotation by checking to see whether the quotation is a verbatim transcription of the original words, but our judgment about the accuracy of a paraphrase or a summary is bound to be more subjective and therefore relative.

Here is a direct quotation from Thomas Babington Macaulay's essay-review of Leopold von Ranke's classic *Ecclesiastical and Politcal History of the Popes of Rome During the Sixteenth and Seventeenth Centuries* (1840) and five attempts to paraphrase a part of, or to summarize the whole of, this passage:

During the eighteenth century, the influence of the Church of Rome was constantly on the decline. Unbelief made extensive conquests in all the Catholic countries of Europe and in some countries obtained a complete ascendancy. The Papacy was at length brought so low as to be an object of derision to infidels and of pity rather than of hatred to Protestants. During the nineteenth century, this fallen Church has been gradually rising from her depressed state and reconquering her old dominion. No person who calmly reflects on what, within the last few years, has passed in Spain, in Italy, in South America, in Ireland, in the Netherlands, in Prussia, even in France, can doubt that the power of this Church over the hearts and minds of men is now greater far than it was when the Encyclopaedia and the Philosophical Dictionary appeared.

1. Macaulay maintains that the influence of the Catholic Church was greater in the nineteenth century than at any other time in its history.

2. During the 1700s, according to Thomas B. Macaulay, the influence of the Catholic Church was constantly on the decline.

3. The Roman Papacy, Macaulay avers, is despised by infidels and hated by Protestants.

4. During the eighteenth century, skepticism, Macaulay says, increased in all the Catholic countries of Europe.

5. Thomas Babington Macaulay's thesis is that although the influence of the Roman Catholic Church declined during the eighteenth century, that Church regained its power in Europe during the nineteenth century.

D

Sentence 1. is an inaccurate paraphrase of the last sentence of the quotation from Macaulay, for what Macaulay said in that final sentence is that the influence of the Catholic Church was greater now in the nineteenth century than it was in the eighteenth century, when the *Encyclopaedia* and the *Philosophical Dictionary* were published.

Sentence 2. is a fairly accurate paraphrase of the first sentence of the original, but the wording and the structure of that paraphrase are so close to the original that this sentence could be regarded as an instance of plagiarism. (See *Plagiarism,* p 184.)

Sentence 3. is a slightly inaccurate paraphrase of Macaulay's third sentence, because, in relation to the original sentence, it states a half-truth: the Papacy was derided by infidels but, according to Macaulay, only during the eighteenth century, and while the Papacy may have been hated by Protestants at an earlier time, it was pitied rather than hated in the eighteenth century. In short, the paraphrase is misleading.

If the word *skepticism* can be regarded as a synonym for Macaulay's *unbelief,* sentence 4. is an accurate paraphrase of the second sentence of the quotation.

Sentence 5. is an accurate summary of the main point of the quotation from Macaulay.

Note the varying degrees of inaccuracy that we have observed in the five translations.

Sample self-contained notecard:

```
010.92                              McCARTHYISM - KOREAN
                                    & VIETNAM WARS
        WHITE, THEODORE H.
IN SEARCH OF HISTORY: A PERSONAL ADVENTURE
     NEW YORK: HARPER, 1978. 395-396


  WHITE SAYS THAT OUR INABILITY TO DEAL EFFECTIVELY
  WITH ASIAN COUNTRIES DURING THE 50s AND 60s
  (KOREA & VIETNAM) WAS THE RESULT OF THE LOSS OF A
  GENERATION OF EXPERIENCED AND DEDICATED FOREIGN
  SERVICE OFFICERS WHO HAD BEEN DISPERSED TO
  OTHER POSTS OR PURGED COMPLETELY.
      (PARAPHRASED - ITALICS ADDED)
```

D

Another method of compiling bibliography and notecards is to keep two sets. One set of cards should contain all of the information needed to compile the *Works Cited* at the end of your paper. The other set, keyed to the author and pages in the upper left-hand corner and the subject heading in the upper right-hand corner, is used to record verbatim, summarized, or paraphrased notes.

Verbatim:

Note that quotation marks have been used to indicate that it is a direct quotation, that the page number between slashes (/110/) shows where the quotation went over from one page to the next, and that the notation "italics added" shows that it was the researcher, not the author, who italicized the work.

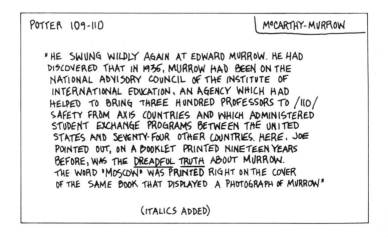

POTTER 109-110   McCARTHY-MURROW

"HE SWUNG WILDLY AGAIN AT EDWARD MURROW. HE HAD
DISCOVERED THAT IN 1935, MURROW HAD BEEN ON THE
NATIONAL ADVISORY COUNCIL OF THE INSTITUTE OF
INTERNATIONAL EDUCATION, AN AGENCY WHICH HAD
HELPED TO BRING THREE HUNDRED PROFESSORS TO /110/
SAFETY FROM AXIS COUNTRIES AND WHICH ADMINISTERED
STUDENT EXCHANGE PROGRAMS BETWEEN THE UNITED
STATES AND SEVENTY-FOUR OTHER COUNTRIES. HERE, JOE
POINTED OUT, ON A BOOKLET PRINTED NINETEEN YEARS
BEFORE, WAS THE DREADFUL TRUTH ABOUT MURROW.
THE WORD "MOSCOW" WAS PRINTED RIGHT ON THE COVER
OF THE SAME BOOK THAT DISPLAYED A PHOTOGRAPH OF MURROW"

(ITALICS ADDED)

Paraphrased:

WHITE 395-396

MCCARTHYISM—
KOREAN & VIETNAM WARS

WHITE SAYS THAT OUR INABILITY TO DEAL
EFFECTIVELY WITH ASIAN COUNTRIES DURING
THE 50s AND 60s (KOREA AND VIETNAM) WAS
THE RESULT OF THE LOSS OF A GENERATION OF
EXPERIENCED AND DEDICATED FOREIGN SERVICE
OFFICERS WHO HAD BEEN DISPERSED TO OTHER
POSTS <u>OR</u> PURGED COMPLETELY.

(ITAL. ADDED)

E   Incorporating Sources

WHAT NEEDS TO BE DOCUMENTED?

As you draft your paper, you will have to develop a sense
for what needs to be documented. Here are some guidelines to help you:

1. Any direct quotation should be followed by a citation of the
source. Be sure to enclose the quotation in quotation marks.

2. Paraphrased material may or may not need to be followed by a
parenthetical citation of the source. If, for instance, the fact or
information that you report in your own words is *generally*

E

known by people knowledgeable on the subject, you probably would not have to document that paraphrased material. For example, if you were writing a research paper on the assassination of Abraham Lincoln, you ordinarily would not have to document your statement that John Wilkes Booth shot Lincoln in Ford's Theater in Washington in April of 1865, because that historical fact is common knowledge. But if one of the arguments in your paper concerned the *exact time of the day* when he was shot, you would have to document your statement that Lincoln was shot at 8:40 P.M. on the evening of April 14, 1865. When, however, you cannot resolve your doubt about whether paraphrased material needs to be documented, document it.

3. When you are summarizing, in your own words, a great deal of information that you have gathered from your reading, you can be spared having to document several sentences in that summary by using a *content endnote*. (See the discussion on p. 192 regarding the proper use and format of endnotes.)

PLAGIARISM

If you present as your own words what you have copied from some other author or if you present some paraphrased material without acknowledging the source of the data or information, you are guilty of plagiarism. (See the section on *Accuracy in Notes,* p. 178, for some examples of acceptable and unacceptable paraphrases.) The academic community regards plagiarism as a very serious offense, punishable by a failing grade on the paper or by a failing grade in the course or by dismissal from school. If you value your personal integrity and your status in school, you should resist the temptation to engage in this kind of intellectual dishonesty. For what needs to be documented in a paper, see the three guidelines presented in the previous section.

KEEP QUOTATIONS TO A MINIMUM

A research paper should not be just a pastiche of long quotations stitched together by an occasional comment or by a transitional sentence by the author of the paper. You should use your own words as much as possible, and when you do quote, you should keep the quotation brief. Often a quoted phrase or sentence will make a point more emphatically than a long quotation. You must learn to look for the phrase or sentence that represents the kernel of the quotation and to use that extract rather than the full quotation. Otherwise, the point you want to make with the quotation may be lost in all the verbiage. You will be more likely to keep your quotations short if you try to work most of them into the framework of your own sentence, like this:

> The *New York Times* claims that the recent increase in enrollments at community colleges across the nation is "the main reason that total enrollment in higher education has not fallen, as educational forecasters expected would happen by now" (Maeroff).

Sometimes, however, when you find it difficult to present the essential point in a short extract, you will have to quote something at greater length. Long quotations (two sentences or more) should be *inset* ten spaces from the left-hand margin, with *no quotation marks enclosing the quotation,* and *triple-spaced* between the long quotation and the rest of the text, like this:

```
To support his contention, Carl Sagan cites

an empirical study that was done to determine

the most common varieties of dreams:

        Statistical studies have been made
```

```
of the most common categories of
dreams——studies which, at least to
some extent, ought to illuminate
the nature of dreams.  In a survey
of the dreams of college students,
the following were, in order, the
five most frequent types: (1)
falling; (2) being pursued or
attacked; (3) attempting repeatedly
and unsuccessfully to perform a
task; (4) various academic learning
experiences; and (5) diverse sexual
experiences (164—165).
```

ELLIPSIS PERIODS

Ellipsis periods (three spaced periods) are used to indicate that a word or several words or whole sentences have been omitted from a direct quotation:

> The president said last week that "the American people . . . would not tolerate such violence."

(Note that there is a space between periods; wrong form:...)
The three spaced periods indicate that a string of words has been omitted. To show the deletion of whole sentences, insert the ellipsis, while retaining the original punctuation (the period immediately after the word *context* below is the usual period that marks the end of a sentence):

These results have no connection with any genuine attempt to use words in a normally expected context. . . . A similar artificial monstrosity could be contrived by jumbling together inappropriate metaphors.

Usually there is no need to put ellipsis periods at the beginning or end of a quotation, because the reader knows that the quotation has been extracted from a larger context. Reserve ellipsis periods for indicating omissions *within* quotations. Take care that such omissions do not destroy the original meaning or intent of the passage.

SQUARE BRACKETS

Square brackets are used to enclose anything that the author of the research paper inserts into a direct quotation:

About this tendency to indulge in scatological language, H. A. Taine wrote, "He [Swift] drags poetry not only through the mud, but into the filth; he rolls in it like a raging madman, he enthrones himself in it, and bespatters all passers-by."

The Senator was emphatic in stating his reaction to the measure: "This action by HEW [Health, Education, and Welfare] will definitely not reverse the downward spiral [of prices and wages] that has plagued us for the last eight months."

We find this entry in the Japanese admiral's diary: "Promptly at 8:32 on Sunday morning of December 6 [*sic*], 1941, I dispatched the first wave of bombers for the raid on Perl Harber. [*sic*]."

(**Sic** *is a Latin adverb meaning "thus," "in this manner," and is used to let the reader know that the error in logic or fact or grammar or spelling in the quotation has been copied exactly as it was in the original source. It is italicized because it is a foreign word.*)

If your typewriter does not have keys that make square

E

brackets, you will have to draw the brackets with a pen after you remove the paper from the typewriter, and so you should leave spaces for the brackets.

F   Documenting Sources—MLA System

In the second edition of the *MLA Handbook for Writers of Research Papers,* edited by Joseph Gibaldi and Walter S. Achtert and published in the autumn of 1984, and in the subsequently published *The MLA Style Manual* (1985), the Modern Language Association (MLA) presented its radical change in the style of documenting research papers that had been standard for most books and journals in the humanities since the first edition of the *MLA Style Sheet* appeared in 1951. Instead of indicating the source of quotations and citations in footnotes or in endnotes, the MLA system now uses a parenthetical style of documentation, much like the APA system (see the details of the APA system on pp. 209–212. The MLA Committee on Research Activities believes that this new system of documentation is characterized by "precision, accuracy, economy, consistency, clarity, and comprehensibility" and that it will help to bridge the gap that had existed between the documentation system of the humanities and that of other disciplines.

The two substantive consequences of the change are (1) that footnotes or endnotes are no longer used to indicate the source of quotations and citations that appear in the text of a research paper and (2) that all researched essays— even those published in professional journals—carry a bibliography of all the works cited in the paper. The essence of the new style of documentation is that some kind of lead-in in the text tells the reader that a quotation or citation or allusion is about to be presented and that a brief reference presented in parentheses tells the reader where to look in the *Works Cited* page for full bibliographical information about the source of that quotation, citation, or allusion.

There are other, mainly mechanical, changes in the new MLA style of documentation:

1. Arabic numerals, rather than Roman numerals, are used to indicate the volume numbers of books as well as journals. (Roman numerals, however, will still be used (a) to identify a person in a series—e.g., Henry VIII, Pope John XXIII; (b) to cite the pages in the preliminary section of a book—e.g., viii, xiv; (c) to designate some conventional references—e.g., (*Hamlet* IV ii 25–30, *PL* VI 160–2).

2. The abbreviations **p.** (for *page*) and **pp.** (for *pages*) have been eliminated before page numbers, even when no volume number is given.

3. The abbreviations **l.** (for *line*) and **ll.** (for *lines*) have been eliminated before line numbers.

4. The comma after the title of a journal has been eliminated—e.g., *German Quarterly* 34 (1961): 78–82.

5. A colon separates the volume number (and date) from the page number—e.g., 97 (1962): 318–24 or 2:57.

6. For journals that begin each issue with page 1, the volume number *and* issue number are given—e.g., *American-German Review* 20.4 (1954): 9–10. Sometimes, however, it might be desirable to give the month or the season also—e.g., 58.2 (May 1964):113–4, or 30.3 (Winter 1945): 87.

7. The place of publication is given as it is spelled on the title page or the copyright page. Therefore, sometimes the foreign name of a city rather than the Anglicized name is given in the bibliographical reference—e.g., *Praha* for Prague, *München* for Munich, *Braunschweig* for Brunswick. (In some cases, however,

F

it might be useful to give the Anglicized spelling of the city in brackets—e.g., *Köln* [Cologne].)

MODEL PARENTHETICAL CITATIONS

The general principle governing parenthetical documentation is that only as much additional information should be given within the parentheses as is necessary to enable the reader to determine the source of the quotation or citation or allusion. For instance, if the lead-in for a quotation in the text supplies the name of the author and if only one work by that author is given on the *Works Cited* page at the end of the paper, only the page number of the quoted works needs to be given in the parentheses. (See the first of the following examples.)

1. Author Cited in the Lead-in:
Travis says that jazz was incubated in Chicago even though it was not conceived there (8–9).

2. Author Not Cited in the Lead-in:
Jazz was incubated in Chicago, even though it was not conceived there (Travis 8–9).

3. Two or Three Authors:
Logan and Cohen credit the Niagara Movement with being the first successful organized effort to voice the Negro protest in the twentieth century (164).

4. More Than Three Authors:
"Popular sovereignty" meant that settlers could vote for or against slavery at the first meeting of their territorial legislature (Divine et al. 384–85).

5. Unknown Authorship:
In architecture, integration of the arts should complement the architectural forms and enhance the total environment (Conrad Schmitt Studios).

F

6. Two or More Works by the Same Author:

"Hollywood, or a segment of it at least, was becoming increasingly active on the question of civil rights" (Baldwin, *No Name in the Street* 132).

"Some argue that a people cannot have a future until they accept their past" (Baldwin, *The Fire Next Time* 95).

[**Note:** Shortened versions of titles are acceptable—e.g., *No Name* or *Fire*.]

7. Multivolume Work:

Other and more serious problems than transportation were raised by the westward movement after the war (Morison & Commager 1:441).

8. Government Document or Corporate Author:

The Commission on Law Enforcement and Administration of Justice concluded that there is far more crime than is ever reported (v).

9. A Novel:

Melville's narrator describes Captain Ahab as having "an eternal anguish in his face . . ." (90; ch. 28).

10. A Poem:

An example of personification is Tennyson's "broad stream in his banks complaining . . ." (*Shalott* 3.120).

11. A Play:

They were, in fact, "a pair of star-crossed lovers" (*Romeo and Juliet* Prologue.6).

12. An Interview:

When questioned about how wise it is for actors to take work doing commercials, my friend expressed no concern that the practice would jeopardize his career (Lordan).

F

13. Citing an Entire Work:
(When citing an entire work, rather than just a part of the
work, it is preferred that the author's name be included in
the text—*not* in a parenthetical reference.)

Fleming uses this kind of approach throughout *Arts & Ideas.*

ENDNOTES/FOOTNOTES

In cases where several sources are cited and it is necessary
to indicate volume numbers, page numbers, multiple authors, etc., an endnote (or footnote) should be used.
Clearly, the following citation would be intrusive and dis-
ruptive in your text:

(Holmes 118–22; Sims and Bates 1:233–34; Whitfield iv–vii;
Ray 97; Scott et al. 512–14)

A superscript numeral is used in the text to direct the reader to the page titled **Notes** at the end of the paper or to a
footnote that appears at the bottom of the page.

Two or more works can be included in a single parenthetical reference simply by separating them with a semicolon:

(Keplar 616; Woolwine 97–99)

G   The Works Cited Page—MLA Style

GENERAL INSTRUCTIONS

In a research paper, the bibliography is placed at the end of
the paper. It is here that the researcher provides full information about all the sources used in the paper. Start the list
on a new page and proceed as follows:

1. The heading **Bibliography** or **Works Cited** should be centered, one inch down from the top of the page.

2. Double-space between the heading and the first entry.

3. Begin the first entry flush with the left-hand margin. If an entry requires more than one line, indent all subsequent lines five spaces from the left margin.

4. Double-space between *and* within entries and continue the list for as many pages as necessary.

Alphabetize the entries by the author's last name or, if the work is anonymous, according to the first letter of the first significant word in the title. For example, *A Handbook of Korea* is alphabetized under "H."

MODEL *WORKS CITED* ENTRIES

1. A Single Book by a Single Author:
Seki, Hozen. *The Great Natural Way.* New York: American Buddhist Academy, 1976.

2. A Single Book by More Than One Author:
Baran, Paul A., and Paul M. Sweezy. *Monopoly Capital: An Essay on American Economic and Social Order.* New York: Monthly Review P, 1966.

3. A Book of More Than One Volume:
Hays, William Lee, and Robert L. Winkler. *Statistics: Probability, Inference, and Decision.* 2 vols. New York: Holt, 1970.

4. A Book Edited by One or More Editors:
Coats, Alfred W., and Ross M. Robertson, eds. *Essays in American Economic History.* London: Edward Arnold, 1969.

Smith, David Nichol, ed. *The Letters of Jonathan Swift to Charles Ford.* Oxford: Clarendon P, 1935.

5. An Essay or a Chapter by an Author in an Edited Collection:

Svaglic, Martin J. "Classical Rhetoric and Victorian Prose." *The Art of Victorian Prose.* Ed. George Levine and William Madden. New York: Oxford UP, 1968. 268–88.

6. A New Edition of a Book:

Doughty, Oswald. *A Victorian Romantic, Dante Gabriel Rossetti.* 2nd ed. London: Oxford UP, 1960.

7. A Book That Is Part of a Series:

Heytesbury, William. *Medieval Logic and the Rise of Mathematical Physics.* University of Wisconsin Publications in Medieval Science. No. 3. Madison: U of Wisconsin P, 1956.

8. A Book in a Paperback Series:

Wilson, Edmund. *To the Finland Station.* Anchor Books. Garden City, NY: Doubleday, 1955.

9. A Translation:

Dostoevsky, Fyodor. *Crime and Punishment.* Constance Garnet, trans. New York: Heritage, 1938.

10. A Signed and an Unsigned Article from an Encyclopedia:

Ewing, J. A. "Steam-Engine and Other Heat-Engines." *Encyclopaedia Britannica.* 9th ed. 1980.

"Dwarfed Trees." *Encyclopedia Americana.* 1948.

11. An Article from a Journal:

Adkins, Nelson. "Emerson and the Bardic Tradition." *Publications of the Modern Language Association* 72 (1948): 662–67.

12. An Article in a Popular Magazine:
Levin, Robert J. "Sex, Morality, and Society." *Saturday Review* 9 July
1966. 29–30.

13. A Signed and an Unsigned Article in a Newspaper:
Van Matre, Lynn. "Evergreen Rockers: '60s stars built to last." *Chicago
Tribune* 12 Jan. 1986, final ed.: 13:20.

"Panel says FDA not doing its job." *Chicago Tribune* 13 Jan. 1986, Chica-
goland ed.: 8.

14. A Signed Book Review:
Dalbor, John B. Rev. of *Meaning and Mind: A Study in the Psychology of
Language,* by Robert F. Terwilliger. *Philosophy & Rhetoric* 5 (1972):
60–61.

15. A Government Booklet or Pamphlet:
United States. Social Security Administration. *Aid to Families with Depen-
dent Children: 1973 Recipient Characteristics Study.* Publication No.
(SSA). 77–11777. June 1975.

16. A Personal Letter or Interview:
Glenn, Senator John. Letter to the author. 20 June 1983.

Herrens, Malcolm B. Telephone interview. 3 February 1980.

17. A Recording or Jacket Notes:
Seeger, Pete, and Arlo Guthrie. "Joe Hill." *Together in Concert.* Warner,
HR 3120, 1975.

18. A Film, a Radio Program, or a Television Program:
Tootsie. With Dustin Hoffman, Jessica Lange, and Teri Garr. Writ. Don
McGuire and Larry Gelbart. Dir. Sydney Pollack. A Mirage/Punch
Production. Columbia, 1982.

G

H   Model Research Paper—MLA Style

Katrina Wolcott Kelley

Professor Zilversmit

American Studies 210

November, 1987

Radicalism in the Federal Theatre Project

During the Great Depression

"I don't know why I still hang on to the idea that unemployed actors get just as hungry as anybody else," said Harry Hopkins in 1934, when he asked Hallie Flanagan to be head of the Works Progress Administration's (WPA) Federal Theatre Project (Flanagan 8-9). When Ms. Flanagan accepted the job, the federal government was launched into its first venture as a theatrical "angel." The purposes of the Project were to employ theatre people who were on welfare (or on "relief," as it was called in those days), to create new audiences for live theatre, and to bring "to people across America, hitherto unable to afford dramatic entertainment, a theatre which should reflect our country, its history, its

H

present problems, its diverse regions and populations
(Flanagan 45). Ninety percent of the people who were
employed by the project were to be from the relief rolls, and
each employee was to be paid $23.86 a week regardless of his
or her job (Lloyd). There were to be separate units for each
type of production. In New York City, for instance, there
were five large units, each with its own theatre: the Living
Newspaper, the Popular Price Theatre (25—50¢ admission, with
original plays by new authors), the Experimental Theatre, the
Negro Theatre, and the Tryout Theatre. Later, there was a
Children's Theatre. Between its establishment in August,
1934, and its sudden termination in June, 1939, the Federal
Theatre Project (FTP) employed thousands of people—at one
time, over 12,000 people (Walsh and Bowers 1).

In 1974, two young professors from George Mason
University in Fairfax, Virginia, discovered a treasure house
of Federal Theatre Project material in an abandoned airplane
hangar near Baltimore, Maryland; the U.S. Library of Congress
placed this valuable cache of information on permanent loan
at George Mason University, which has established a Research
Center for the Federal Theatre Project (Walsh and Bowers 2).
One of the projects of that Research Center has been to
record interviews with many of the actors, playwrights,

H

directors, and designers who were once associated with the
Project. Three of the people whose reminiscences about those
days in the 1930s were recorded on cassette tape were Will
Geer, Carlton Moss, and John Randolph. Because the Federal
Theatre Project was terminated in 1939, accused of being a
monstrous boondoggle and alleged to be a radical organization
producing subversive plays, I was particularly interested in
hearing these men's feelings and thoughts about the political
action, the censorship, the charges of Communist
infiltration, and the fortunes of blacks associated with the
theatre group during those dark days of the Great Depression.
Were the charges of subversive radicalism true? Was the
country in those days ever in serious danger of being
undermined by the "Reds" who were associated with the Federal
Theatre Project?

John Randolph remembers his experiences with the Project
as being the education of a young man. Speaking in a
cultured, mellow voice, with an occasional lapse into
"Bronxese," Randolph recalls his youth as a young actor named
Mortimer Lipman, active in a left-wing group called the
Theatre Collective.

He recalls those days in these words:

H

My stepfather lost his business as a furrier, and
he just disappeared like a lot of men did in those
days. So my mother was left with my brother and
myself, and she supported us by playing cards two
afternoons a week. The ladies would meet at her
house, and she'd charge like eight dollars for
coffee, fruit, and cake. . . . She was a good
card-player, and she kept us alive that way while
we were looking for my father. He'd disappeared
because the gangsters were after him. He'd
borrowed money. Then he took a job selling soda on
a truck, and when that failed, he just disappeared,
and we went on home relief.

Some time after the family went on relief, Randolph was
invited to join the FTP. "It was all so exciting to me," he
says, "to be able to get paid $23.86, to get my family off
home relief--and I was able to support my family on that
$23.86 a week--and to do work that I was interested in and to
do it consistently."

As a member of the Children's Theatre Unit in New York
City, Randolph was sent at one point to the Maine Unit to

H

play the leading man in <u>Sure Fire</u>. He had never been out of the Bronx before, and Maine was another world to him. The audience in Maine had not seen a live show for a long time--if ever. He remembers that "at the end of the first act, they left! They didn't know to come back; they thought that was the whole play. We learned to have a juggler or a tap dancer come out immediately to keep the audience there."

Keeping the audience in the theatre was a problem back in New York City too. The almost aborted production of Marc Blitzstein's opera, <u>The Cradle Will Rock</u>, in June, 1937, is probably the most remembered single event of the Federal Theatre's four short years. Produced by John Houseman and Orson Welles, the opera elicited all the paranoia that the government felt about the Project. Blitzstein remembers his opera as being "hot stuff politically," because it dealt with America's struggle for unionism in the steel industry, at a time when a combine called "Little Steel" had its union troubles constantly featured in the daily newspapers. The opera was also controversial because it dealt with prostitution, "literal prostitution," Blitzstein says, "set against the background of prostitution of another kind: the sell-out of one's profession, one's talents, one's dignity

and integrity at the hands of big business or the powers
that be."

Because of pressure from U.S. Steel, according to
Blitzstein, government officials in Washington refused
permission for the show to be put on. One participant
recalls the incident vividly:

> Equity said we had no contract and if we played,
> we'd be thrown out of our trade unions and the
> Federal Theatre. . . . We decided to do the show
> anyway. . . . Houseman and Welles asked some of us
> to go out front and hold the audience--because it
> was a beautiful, packed audience. I did all the
> songs I knew from <u>Cradle</u> and also little quotations
> from Mark Twain and Walt Whitman and everything
> under the sun (Geer).

According to Marc Blitzstein's recollections of this
incident, the actors, musicians, and technicians were told
that if they left the theatre, they would not be allowed back
in. So Houseman gave the young production manager a
ten-dollar bill to commandeer a truck and circle the block

with it until a piano and a theatre could be located. When
the much larger Venice Theatre was found to be available, the
audience rose and began parading up Broadway and Seventh
Avenue, led by the truck and by taxis holding Houseman,
Welles, and Abe Feder, the lighting man. On the way, the
audience doubled in size to almost two thousand people. In
order to protect their jobs, Welles suggested that the actors
buy tickets to get into the theatre and to perform their
roles from the audience. With Blitzstein as the only
musician at a piano on stage and with Feder spotlighting each
actor in the audience, the spontaneous show that followed was
a great success and was greeted by an applauding, cheering
audience, packed in the aisles. Geer recalls, "It was very
exciting because we were defying authority, defying our trade
unions, defying the United States government, defying U.S.
Steel, and our own social order. Very exciting!"

John Randolph feels that the government officials in
Washington did not really expect anything like this to happen
with the Project. He says, "I think they just set the units
all up and figured, what the hell, we'll put some money in
circulation and get people working again. . . . It was a
great political awakening--being with other actors, being

with politically aware people, and becoming aware of
injustice."

Will Geer recalls <u>his</u> political consciousness being
developed during his years with the Project. "I think
theatre helps you become interested in politics and life," he
says. "Politics is part of life, and the theatre should
always hold a mirror up to life." When asked whether there
were any Communists in the Federal Theatre Project, Geer
replied as follows:

> I never attended any cells where I saw any. We'd
> have study groups and lectures on the theatre, and
> I dare say there were Communists there. . . .
> Actually, I knew all the people who were Communists
> myself, personally, because my grandmother-in-law,
> Mother Bloor, was the grande dame of the Communist
> Party. Very amiable, nice, little Quaker-type
> lady, you could hear for ten blocks when she spoke.

When John Randolph was asked about the Communists
associated with the FTP, he said that Communists were
interwoven throughout the fabric of American life in those

days, "and the Communists," he said, "were the first ones to demonstrate for unemployment insurance and home relief, all of which were considered un—American. But he found the Communists to be very "principled people." "I didn't hear anyone telling me to take a bomb and overthrow the government. . . . I think the Communists were constructive, not destructive, not evil people."

The Federal Theatre Project was never integrated. The Negro Theatre Unit was black, and the other units were white. The reason that John Houseman (who was white) was hired to be the head of the Negro Unit in New York was that blacks trusted him (Moss). "Since Houseman was not native—born," says Moss, "he was less likely to be a racist. And he was the man who could get the stuff. He could go downtown and not be thrown off the elevator, not be insulted before he got in the building."

Carlton Moss feels that the play which best reflected the needs of blacks was <u>Conjur Man Dies</u>. At a time of extraordinarily high unemployment, the numbers game flourished in black communities like New York's Harlem, and the conjur man, voodoo, and superstition were closely associated with the numbers game. But the Negro Unit's play which was best remembered was the <u>Voodoo Macbeth</u>, set in

Haiti in 1815. As Norman Lloyd, an actor in the Federal
Theatre, says, "If a black singer sings just a popular song,
it suddenly becomes a black song. That's what happened with
<u>Macbeth</u>. They took it over. . . . There was a kind of voodoo
raciness and a black pulse to it, which you'd never
experience as a Scottish melodrama."

Although it is easy to understand why the Living
Newspaper, Voodoo Shakespeare, and agit-prop opera were
controversial, one would not expect the Children's Theatre
Unit to be charged with radicalism. John Randolph, however,
claims that <u>The Revolt of the Beavers</u>, a play staged for
children, was the only really radical production that the
Federal Theatre Project put on. Dealing with good beavers
and bad beavers, the play turned out to be a political
allegory much like George Orwell's <u>Animal Farm</u>. The editors
of one weekly magazine were more shocked than edified by the
production:

> Believing that plays for children should have a
> moral significance, the Federal Theatre has
> conscientiously produced a revolutionary bedtime
> story, "The Revolt of the Beavers." . . . In the
> form of a Mother Goose fantasy, it is a primer

K. Kelley 11

 lesson in the class struggle. . . . To the kiddies

 of New York, the battle of the laboring classes

 against the sleek and obese chieftains of property

 may be a little too remote. . . . Many children

 now unschooled in the technique of revolution now

 have an opportunity, at Government expense, to

 improve their tender minds. Mother Goose is no

 longer a rhymed escapist. She has been studying

 Marx ("Once Upon a Time").

Charges that not even impressionable children were

immune to the radical preachings of the Communist subversives

contributed to the mounting opposition to the Federal Theatre

Project, and in June of 1939, after a Congressional

investigation, the Project was terminated. Was the FTP as

politically and socially dangerous as its opponents claimed

it was? Listening to the reminiscences on tape of the three

gentle old men, one finds it difficult to imagine how the

productions of this government—sponsored organization could

have been considered a threat to the American way of life.

There were explicit protests in the plays against social injustices, to be sure, but considering the difficult economic conditions of the times, the protests strike us as being tame rather than explosive, corrective rather than subversive. As Howard Taubman, historian of the American theatre, put it, "The plays [the FTP] produced hardly ever ventured beyond the position of the Democratic Party's liberal wing" (233). The Living Newspaper productions seemed to be good examples of that political temper. In fact, Fortune magazine said at the time that Republicans viewed Triple A Plowed Under and Power, two productions of the Living Magazine group, as simply subsidized New Deal propaganda (Mathews 119). Perhaps it is a compliment to the power of theatre that it can be seen as a threatening force. In any case, the Federal Theatre Project did what it set out to do. It employed thousands of theatre people who were on relief and brought a wide diversity and quality of drama, dance, opera, and circus to eager audiences across this land. All in all, it seems to have been more culturally beneficial than politically or socially damaging.

Works Cited

Blitzstein, Marc. "Marc Blitzstein Discusses His Theatre
    Compositions." Spoken Arts Recording No. 717.

Flanagan, Hallie. <u>Arena</u>. New York: Benjamin Blom, 1965.

Geer, Will. Interview by Diane Bowers. On file at the
    Research Center for the Federal Theatre Project. George
    Mason University, Fairfax, VA: 1 June 1976.

Lloyd, Norman. Interview by John O'Connor. On file at the
    Research Center for the Federal Theatre Project. George
    Mason University, Fairfax, VA: 5 January 1976.

Mathews, Jane Dehart. <u>The Federal Theatre 1935–1939: Plays,
    Relief, and Politics</u>. Princeton, NJ: Princeton UP,
    1967.

Moss, Carlton. Interview by Lorraine Brown. On file at the
    Research Center for the Federal Theatre Project. George
    Mason University, Fairfax, VA: 6 August 1976.

"Once Upon a Time." <u>The Saturday Evening Post</u>, 26 June 1937:
    22.

Randolph, John. Interview by Diane Bowers. On file at the
    Research Center for the Federal Theatre Project. George
    Mason University, Fairfax, VA: 28 May 1976.

Taubman, Howard. <u>The Making of the American Theatre</u>. New
    York: Coward McCann, 1965.

Walsh, Elizabeth and Diane Bowers. "WPA Federal Theatre
    Project." <u>Theatre News</u>. 8 (April 1976): 1–3.

H

I Format of the Research Paper: The APA System of Documentation

Just as the MLA system of documentation, illustrated in the previous section, is predominant in the humanities, the American Psychological Association (APA) system is predominant in such fields as psychology, education, psycholinguistics, and many of the social sciences. Over two hundred scholarly journals in the United States now prescribe the APA style of documentation. The highlights of this system will be presented here; for a fuller treatment, consult the readily available paperback edition of *Publication Manual of the American Psychological Association*, 3rd ed. Washington, D.C.: American Psychological Association, 1983.

The principal difference between the MLA and the APA systems is that the MLA in-text and parenthetical citations feature the name of the author and the location of the information; the APA citations feature the name of the author, the *date*, and the location. The date is featured in scientific writing for the obvious reason that a researcher must present the most up-to-date information that is available.

Here is how the first reference to a book would be documented, first in the MLA style and then in the APA style. (Note that the APA in the parentheses retains the abbreviations "p." and "pp." and puts a comma between the author's name and the date of publication.)

1. Author Cited in the Lead-in:
MLA Tracy defended the "big-bang" theory (234).

APA Tracy (1985) defended the "big-bang" theory (p. 234).

2. Author Not Cited in the Lead-in:
MLA The "big-bang" theory can be defended (Tracy 234).

APA The "big-bang" theory can be defended (Tracy, 1985, p. 234).

Readers who wanted fuller information about the work cited in the parenthetical reference could turn to the list of references at the end of the paper. There, in an alphabetical listing, the Tracy work would be entered in double-spaced typescript as follows:

Tracy, Arnold. (1985). *New theories on the origins of the universe.* New York: Downey.

VARIATIONS ON THE BASIC APA STYLE OF DOCUMENTATION

1. If a whole work is being referred to, only the author's last name and the date of the work are given in parentheses.

   A recent study has confirmed that twelve-year-olds grow at an amazingly rapid rate (Swanson, 1969).

2. A page number or a chapter number is supplied only if part of a work is being referred to. Quotations always demand the addition of a page number.

   The committee boldly declared that "morality could not be enforced, but it could be bought" (Dawson, 1975, p. 105).

3. Any information supplied in the text itself need not be repeated in the parentheses.

   Anderson (1948) found that only middle-class Europeans disdained our cultural values.

   In 1965, Miller professed his fervent admiration of our admissions policy.

4. If a work has two authors, both authors should be cited each

time a reference is made to that particular text. If a work has three or more authors, all the authors should be cited the first time, but subsequently only the name of the first author followed by **et al.** needs to be given.

The circulation of false rumors poisoned the environment of that conference (Getty & Howard, 1979).

The overall effect of the smear tactics was a marked decline in voter registrations (Abraham, Davis, & Keppler, 1952).

In three successive national elections, voters from Slavic neighborhoods showed a 72% turnout (Abraham et al., 1952, pp. 324–327).

If several works are cited at the same point in the text, the works should be arranged alphabetically according to the last name of the first author and should be separated with semicolons.

All the studies of the problem agree that the proposed remedy is worse than the malady (Brown & Turkell, 1964; Firkins, 1960; Howells, 1949; Jackson, Miller, & Naylor, undated; Kameron, in press).

If several works by the same author are cited in the same reference, the works are distinguished by the publication dates, arranged in chronological order and separated with commas. Two or more works published by the same author in the same year are distinguished by the letters **a, b, c,** etc., added to the repeated date. In such chronological listings, works "in press" are always listed last.

A consistent view on this point has been repeatedly expressed by the Canadian member of the Commission (Holden, 1959, 1965, 1970, 1971a, 1971b, 1976).

If no author is given for a work, two or three words from

another part of the entry (usually from the title) should be used to refer to the work.

The voters' apathy was decried in the final spring meeting of the city council ("The Gradual Decline," 1976).

LIST OF REFERENCES

The *References* page appended to a paper that observes the APA style is comparable to, and yet different from, the *Works Cited* page in a paper that observes the MLA style. Both systems give full bibliographic information about the works cited in the body of the writing, and both systems arrange the entries alphabetically according to the last name of the author. In both systems, the names of the authors are inverted (surname first), but in the APA system, only the initials of first and middle names are given, and when there are two or more authors for a work, the names of *all* the authors are inverted.

The conventions of sequence, punctuation, and capitalization in the APA style for the *References* section can most easily be illustrated with examples.

1. A Book by a Single Author:

Luria, A. R. (1973). <u>The</u> <u>working</u> <u>brain:</u>   <u>An</u> <u>introduction</u> <u>to</u> <u>neuro-psychology</u>. London: Penguin.

Note that the title of the book is underlined but that only the first word of the title and the first word following the colon in the title are capitalized. (Any proper nouns in a title would also be capitalized; see the following example.) The three main parts of an entry—author, title, and publication data—are separated with periods. Also note that you should leave *two* spaces after the colon separating the place of publication and the name of the publisher.

2. A Book by Several Authors:

Koslin, S., Koslin, B. L., Pargament, R., & Pendelton, S. (1975). <u>An evaluation of fifth grade reading programs in ten New York City Community School Districts, 1973–1974.</u> New York: Riverside Research Institute.

Note that the names of all the authors are inverted, that the names are separated with commas, and that an ampersand (**&**) is put before the last name in the series (even when there are only two names; see the following example.)

3. An Article in an Edited Collection:

Bobrow, D. G., & Norman, D. A. (1975). Some principles of memory schemata. In D. G. Bobrow & A. M. Collins (Eds.), <u>Representation and Understanding</u>: Studies in cognitive science. New York: Academic Press.

Note that the title of the article (**Some principles** etc.) is not enclosed in quotation marks and that only the first word of this title is capitalized. (Any proper nouns in the title of the article would, of course, be capitalized.) Note also that the subsequent names of the two editors (**Eds.**) of the collection are not inverted and that there is no comma between the names.

I

4. An Article in a Journal:

Stahl, A. (1977). The structure of children's compositions: Developmental and ethnic differences. <u>Research in the Teaching of English, 11,</u> 156–163.

Note that all substantive words in the title of the journal are capitalized and that the title of the journal is underlined. Note also that the year comes after the author's name and that the volume number (*11*) is underlined. For a journal that begins the numbering of its pages with page 1 in each issue, the number of the issue should be indicated with an Arabic number following the volume number—*11*(**3**).

5. A Book by a Corporate Author:

American Psychological Association. (1966). <u>Standards for educational and psychological tests and manuals</u>. Washington, DC: Author.

Books and articles with corporate authors are listed alphabetically according to the first significant word of the entry (here **American**). The word **Author** indicates that the publisher of the work is the same as the group named in the author slot. If however, the publisher is different from the corporate author, the name of that publisher would be given right after the place of publication.

These five models cover most of the kinds of published material likely to be used in a research paper. For additional models, consult the *Publication Manual of the American Psychological Association* (3rd ed.).

For an illustration of the physical appearance, in typescript, of a research paper and of a *References* page done according to the APA system of documentation, see the following pages, taken from a twenty-one-page article by Carl Bereiter of the Ontario Institute for Studies in Education: "Development in Writing," in *Testing, Teaching and Learning* (Washington, D.C.: National Institute of Education, 1979), pp. 146–166. This article was later reprinted in L. W. Gregg and E. R. Steinberg, eds., *Cognitive Processes in Writing* (Hillsdale, N.J.: Erlbaum, 1979).

DEVELOPMENT IN WRITING

Carl Bereiter

Although there is a substantial body of data on the
development of writing skills, it has not seemed to have much
implication for instruction. Reviews of writing research
from an educational perspective have given scant attention to
it (Blount, 1973; Braddock, Lloyd-Jones, & Schoer, 1963;
Lyman, 1929; West, 1967). Generally speaking, developmental
research has educational significance only when there is a
conceptual apparatus linking it with questions of practical
significance.

Almost all of the data on writing development consist of
frequency counts--words per communication unit, incidence of
different kinds of dependent clauses, frequency of different
types of writing at different ages, and so on. The conceptual
frameworks used for interpreting these data have come largely
from linguistics (e.g., Hunt, 1965; Loban, 1976; O'Donnell,
Griffin, & Norris, 1967). However informative these analyses
might be to the student of language development, they are

disappointing from an educational point of view. The
variables they look at seem unrelated to commonly held
purposes of writing instruction (Nystrand, 1977).

The purpose of this paper is to synthesize findings on
the growth of writing skills within what may be called an
"applied cognitive-developmental" framework. Key issues
within an applied cognitive-developmental framework are the
cognitive strategies children use and how these are adapted
to their limited information processing capacities (Case,
1975, 1978; Klahr & Wallace, 1976; Scardamalia, in press).
Although this paper will not deal with instructional
implications, it will become evident that the issues
considered within an applied cognitive-developmental
framework are relevant to such concerns of writing
instruction as fluency, coherence, correctness, sense of
audience, style, and thought content.

Students' writing will undoubtedly reflect their overall
language development (Loban, 1976; O'Donnell et al., 1967)
and also their level of cognitive development (Collis &

References

Allen, R. L. (1972). English grammars and English grammar.
    New York: Scribner's.

Blount, N. S. Research on teaching literature, language, and
    composition. (1973). In R. M. W. Travers (Ed.), Second
    handbook of research on teaching. Chicago:
    Rand-McNally.

Braddock, R., Lloyd-Jones, R., & Schoer, L. (1963). Research
    in written composition. Champaign, IL: National
    Council of Teachers of English.

Case, R. (1975). Gearing the demands of instruction to the
    developmental capacities of the learner. Review of
    Educational Research, 45(1), 59-87.

Case, R. (1978). Implications of developmental psychology for
    the design of effective instruction. In A. M. Lesgold,
    J. W. Pellegrino, S. D. Fokemma, & R. Glaser (Eds.),
    Cognitive psychology and instruction. Plenum, NY:
    Division of Plenum Publishing Corporation.

Collis, K. F., & Biggs, J. B. (undated). Classroom examples
    of cognitive development phenomena. ERDC Funded Project
    7/41, University of Newcastle.

Gleason, H. A., Jr. (1965). Linguistics and English grammar. New York: Holt, Rinehart & Winston.

Hunt, K. W. (1965). Grammatical structures written at three grade levels. Champaign, IL: National Council of Teachers of English. (Research Report No. 3.)

Klahr, D., & Wallace, J. G. (1976). Cognitive development: An information-processing view. Hillsdale, NJ: Erlbaum.

Loban, W. (1963). The language of elementary school children. Urbana, IL: National Council of Teachers of English. (Research Report No. 1.)

Loban, W. (1966). Problems in oral English. Urbana, IL: National Council of Teachers of English. (Research Report No. 5.)

Loban, W. (1976). Language development: Kindergarten through grade twelve. Urbana, IL: National Council of Teachers of English. (Research Report No. 18.)

Long, R. B. (1961). The sentence and its parts: A grammar of contemporary English. Chicago: University of Chicago Press.

Lyman, R. (1929). Summary of investigations relating to
grammar, language, and composition. Chicago:
University of Chicago. (Supplementary educational
Monographs, No. 36, published in conjunction with The
School Review and The Elementary School Journal.)

Nystrand, M. (1977). Assessing written communication
competence: A textual cognition model. Toronto, Canada:
The Ontario Institute for Studies in Education. (ERIC
Document Reproduction Service No. ED 133 732.)

O'Donnell, R. C., Griffin, W. J., & Norris, R. C. (1967).
Syntax of kindergarten and elementary school children: A
transformational analysis. Champaign, IL: National
Council of Teachers of English. (Research Report No. 8.)

Scardamalia, M. (in press). How children cope with the
cognitive demands of writing. In C. H. Frederiksen,
M. S. Whiteman, & J. F. Dominic (Eds.), Writing: The
nature, development, and teaching of written
communication.

West, W. W. (1967). Written composition. Review of
Educational Research. 37(2), 159—167.

J   Other Documentation Systems

Most of the scholarly disciplines specify the style of documentation that they prefer, and when you begin to major in one of those disciplines, you will be expected to use that style of documentation in the research papers or articles that you write. In the masthead of professional journals, the editor usually indicates what system of documentation authors should observe in the articles they submit for consideration.

Here is a list of the style manuals for a few of the disciplines:

Council of Biology Editors. Style Manual Committee. <u>CBE Style Manual: A Guide for Authors, Editors, and Publishers in the Biological Sciences.</u> 5th ed. Bethesda: Council of Biology Editors, 1983.

American Chemical Society. <u>Handbook for Authors of Papers in American Chemical Society Publications.</u> Washington: American Chemical Society, 1978.

American Mathematical Society. <u>A Manual for Authors of Mathematical Papers.</u> 7th ed. Providence: American Mathematical Society, 1980.

International Steering Committee of Medical Editors. "Uniform Requirements for Manuscripts Submitted to Biomedical Journals." <u>Annals of Internal Medicine</u> 90 (January 1979): 95–99.

American Institute of Physics. Publications Board. <u>Style Manual for Guidance in the Preparation of Papers.</u> 3rd ed. New York: American Institute of Physics, 1978.

FORMS FOR LETTERS

GENERAL INSTRUCTIONS

The one type of writing that most people engage in after leaving school is letter-writing. You will almost certainly write letters to parents, friends, and acquaintances, and you may have to write letters in connection with your job. Occasionally, you may feel compelled to write a letter to the editor of a newspaper or magazine, and sometimes you may write more formal letters to institutions or officials for such purposes as applying for a job, requesting information or service, or seeking redress of some grievance. Although you do not have to be much concerned about the niceties of form when you are writing to intimate friends, you would be well advised to observe the conventions of form and etiquette in letters addressed to people that you do not know well enough to call by their first names.

Format of Familiar Letter

Letters written to acquaintances are commonly referred to as *familiar letters*. Although usually "anything goes" in letters to acquaintances, you should keep in mind that even the most intimate acquaintance is flattered if the author of the letter observes certain amenities of form. Here is a list of the conventions for the familiar letter.

(a) Familiar letters may be written on lined or unlined paper of any size.

(b) Familiar letters may be handwritten and may be written on both sides of the sheet of paper.

(c) The author of the letter usually puts his or her address and the date at the right-hand side of the heading but does not, as in a business letter, put at the left-hand side of the heading the name and address of the person to whom the letter is addressed.

(d) Depending on the degree of intimacy with the addressee, you may use salutations like these: **Dear Mom, Dear Jim, Dear Julie, Dear Ms. Worth**. The salutation is often followed by a comma rather than the more formal colon.

(e) The body of the letter may be written in indented paragraphs, single- or double-spaced.

(f) Depending on the degree of intimacy with the addressee, you may use complimentary closes like these: **Sincerely, Cordially, Affectionately, Yours, Much love, Fondly, As ever**.

(g) Depending on the degree of intimacy with the addressee, you may sign your full name or just a first name or a nickname.

Format of Business Letter

Formal letters addressed to organizations or customers or professionals or executives are commonly called *business letters*. The form of business letters is more strictly prescribed than the form of familiar letters. Models for a business letter appear on pp. 225 and 227. Here is a list of the conventions for the business letter:

(a) Business letters are written on 8½ × 11 unlined paper or on 8½ × 11 paper with a printed letterhead.

(b) Business letters must be typewritten, single-spaced, on one side of the paper only.

(c) In the sample business letter that is typed on printed letterhead stationery (p. 227), the so-called *full block* format of formal business letters is illustrated. Note that in this format, everything—date, address, greeting, text, complimentary close—begins at the left-hand margin. Compare this format with the *semiblock* format of the sample business letter that is typed on plain white paper (p. 225). All the other directions about format (**d, e, f, g, h, i, j**) apply to both kinds of formal business letters.

(d) Flush with the left-hand margin and in single-spaced block form, type the name and address of the person or the organization to whom the letter is written. (The same form will be used in addressing the envelope.)

(e) Two spaces below this inside address and flush with the left-hand margin, type the salutation, followed by a colon. In addressing an organization rather than a specific person in that organization, use salutations like **Dear Sir** or **Gentlemen** or **Dear Madam** or **Ladies**. If you know the name of the person, you should use the last name, prefaced with **Mr.** or **Miss** or **Mrs.** or, if uncertain about the marital status of a woman, **Ms.**—e.g., **Dear Mr. Toler, Dear Miss Cameron, Dear Mrs. Nakamura, Dear Ms. Ingrao**. Women who feel that marital status should be no more specified in their own case than in that of a man (for whom **Mr.** serves, irrespective of whether he is married) prefer **Ms.** to **Mrs.** and **Miss**. The plural of **Mr.** is **Messrs.**; the plural of **Mrs.** or **Ms.** is **Mmes.**; the plural of **Miss** is **Misses**. Professional titles may also be used in the salutation:

Dear Professor Newman, Dear Dr. Marton. (*Webster's New Collegiate Dictionary* carries an extensive list of the forms of address for various dignitaries [judges, clergy, legislators, etc.].)

(f) The body of the letter should be single-spaced, except for double-spacing between paragraphs. Paragraphs are not indented but start flush with the left-hand margin.

(g) The usual complimentary closes for business letters are these: **Sincerely yours, Yours truly, Very truly yours**. The complimentary close is followed by a comma.

(h) Type your name about three or four spaces below the complimentary close. The typed name should not be prefaced with a professional title (**Dr., Rev.**) nor followed with a designation of academic degrees (**M.A., Ph.D.**), but below the typed name, you may indicate your official capacity (**President, Director of Personnel, Managing Editor**). You should sign your name in the space between the complimentary close and the typed name.

(i) If one or more copies of the letter are being sent to others, that fact should be indicated with a notation like the following in the lower left-hand side of the page (**cc** is the abbreviation of **carbon copy**):
cc: Mary Hunter
     Robert Allison

(j) If the letter was dictated to, and typed by, a secretary, that fact should be indicated by a notation like the following, which is typed flush with the left-hand margin and below the signature (the writer's initials are given in capital letters, the secretary's in lowercase): **WLT/cs** or **WLT:cs**.

See the following models for the text and envelope of the two styles of business letters.

Semiblock

239 Riverside Road
Columbus, OH 43210
January 5, 1986

Mr. Thomas J. Weiss
Manager, Survey Division
Acme Engineering Company, Inc.
5868 Fanshawe Drive
Omaha, NB 68131

Dear Mr. Weiss:

Mr. Robert Miller, sales representative of the Rushmore Caterpillar Company of Columbus and a long-time friend of my father, told me that when he saw you at a convention in Chicago recently, you indicated you would have two or three temporary positions open this summer in your division. Mr. Miller kindly offered to write you about me, but he urged me to write also.

By June, I will have completed my junior year in the Department of Civil Engineering at Ohio State University. Not only do I need to work this summer to finance my final year of college, but I also need to get some practical experience in surveying tracts on a large road-building project such as your company is now engaged in. After checking with several of the highway contractors in this area, I have learned that all of them have already hired their quota of engineering students for next summer.

For the last three summers, I have worked for the Worley Building Contractors of Columbus as a carpenter's helper and as a cement-finisher. Mr. Albert Michaels, my foreman for the last three summers, has indicated that he would write a letter of reference for me, if you want one. He understands why I want to get some experience in surveying this summer, but he told me that I would have priority for a summertime job with Worley if I wanted it.

Among my instructors in civil engineering, the two men who know me best are Dr. Theodore Sloan, who says that he knows you, and Mr. A. M. Slater. Currently, I have a 3.2 quality-point average in all my subjects, but I have straight A's in all my engineering courses. For the last two quarters, I have worked as a laboratory assistant for Professor Sloan.

I am anxious to get experience in my future profession, and I am quite willing to establish temporary residence in Omaha during the summer. I own a four-cylinder sub-compact car that I could use to travel to the job site each day. I am in good health, and I would be available to work for long hours and at odd hours during the summer months. If you want any letters of recommendation from any of the men named in my letter, please let me know.

Sincerely yours,

Oscar Jerman
Oscar Jerman

cc: Robert Miller

Business letter typed on plain, unlined paper

Addressed Business-size Envelope

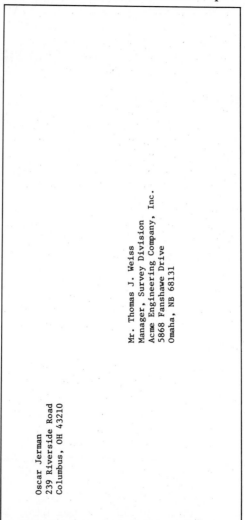

Oscar Jerman
239 Riverside Road
Columbus, OH 43210

Mr. Thomas J. Weiss
Manager, Survey Division
Acme Engineering Company, Inc.
5868 Fanshawe Drive
Omaha, NB 68131

Full Block

EDUCATIONAL ASSOCIATES, INC.   PHONE: 815-727-9452

SUITE 400, RIALTO SQUARE BUILDING   ●   5 EAST VAN BUREN STREET   ●   JOLIET, IL 60431

February 23, 1986

Dr. John A. Whitney
Superintendent
Garden Grove High School
Garden Grove, IL 50488

Dear Dr. Whitney:

The week that my staff and I spent on your campus was an unusually
productive one. It is rare to find both the level of awareness
and the commitment to finding solutions to problems that is
present in the Garden Grove school district.

A report of our findings and recommendations will be available
on March 15. I think we should meet as soon as possible after
that date to review the material it will contain. Perhaps we
can also talk then about the best way to distribute the report.
Some administrators prefer to present our reports themselves --
others find it more appropriate for a member of our staff to
do it. You know better than we do what is best for your district.

I will be in Washington, D.C. from March 13 through March 16.
I will be available at the time most convenient for you after
that.

Please extend our thanks and appreciation to your faculty and
staff, students, parents, and school board members for their
cooperation during our visit to Garden Grove.

Sincerely yours,

Kathleen W. Bolden

Kathleen W. Bolden
President
Educational Associates, Inc.

KWB/ig

cc: Richard K. Rapp
    President, Board of Education
    Garden Grove High School

Business letter on letterhead stationery

Letterhead Business Envelope

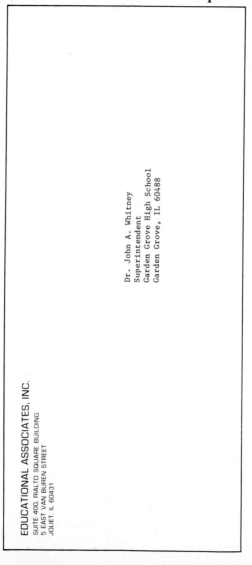

THE TWO-LETTER POSTAL ABBREVIATIONS

Here is the U.S. Postal Service list of two-letter abbreviations of the fifty states, the District of Columbia, and outlying areas. These abbreviations should be set down in capital letters without a period and should be followed by the appropriate five- or nine-digit ZIP code—for example, Glenview, IL 60025–9969.

Alabama	**AL**	Montana	**MT**
Alaska	**AK**	Nebraska	**NE**
Arizona	**AZ**	Nevada	**NV**
Arkansas	**AR**	New Hampshire	**NH**
California	**CA**	New Jersey	**NJ**
Colorado	**CO**	New Mexico	**NM**
Connecticut	**CT**	New York	**NY**
Delaware	**DE**	North Carolina	**NC**
District of Columbia	**DC**	North Dakota	**ND**
Florida	**FL**	Ohio	**OH**
Georgia	**GA**	Oklahoma	**OK**
Guam	**GU**	Oregon	**OR**
Hawaii	**HI**	Pennsylvania	**PA**
Idaho	**ID**	Puerto Rico	**PR**
Illinois	**IL**	Rhode Island	**RI**
Indiana	**IN**	South Carolina	**SC**
Iowa	**IA**	South Dakota	**SD**
Kansas	**KS**	Tennessee	**TN**
Kentucky	**KY**	Texas	**TX**
Louisiana	**LA**	Utah	**UT**
Maine	**ME**	Vermont	**VT**
Maryland	**MD**	Virgin Islands	**VI**
Massachusetts	**MA**	Virginia	**VA**
Michigan	**MI**	Washington	**WA**
Minnesota	**MN**	West Virginia	**WV**
Mississippi	**MS**	Wisconsin	**WI**
Missouri	**MO**	Wyoming	**WY**

A RÉSUMÉ

A résumé (pronounced *REZ-oo-may*) is also referred to by, and sometimes even labeled with, the Latin terms *curriculum vitae* (the course of one's life) or *vita brevis* (a short life) or simply *vita*. Whatever name it bears, this document presents, usually on one or two pages and in the form of a list, a summary of an applicant's job objective, education, work experience, personal experiences, extracurricular activities, achievements, honors, etc. Sent out with a cover letter that is addressed to a specific person in the company, the résumé is intended to introduce the applicant to a potential employer and to elicit a request for further information about the applicant and ultimately for an interview.

Under such headings as *Education*, *Work Experience*, and *Extracurricular Activities*, the items are usually listed in reverse chronological order, starting with the most recent and ending with the earliest. The items that the applicant chooses to list should be pertinent to the kind of job being sought. The cover letter that accompanies the résumé should call attention to those items that are especially pertinent to the particular job that is being applied for.

The résumé and the cover letter should be neatly, flawlessly, and attractively typed on good heavy bond paper. The physical appearance alone of these documents could make a crucial impression on the reader. You cannot afford to be sloppy or careless in preparing these documents. Remember that you are trying to sell yourself and the service you have to offer. So in listing your assets and achievements, do not misrepresent yourself, either by exaggerating or by downplaying your merits. Do not brag; let the facts speak for themselves. For example, if you mention that you have a four-year Grade Point Average of 3.8, you do not have to boast that you have been an excellent student.

The résumé usually mentions that letters of reference and transcripts of academic work are available upon request. In the case of students who are applying for a job, the résumé sometimes gives the address of the school's placement office where the interested employer can write for the applicant's dossier, which is a collection of such documents as transcripts, letters of reference, and samples of one's writing. If your résumé and cover letter move the potential employer to write for your dossier, you will have reached an important stage in the process of applying for a job. The next important step is to gain an invitation to a face-to-face interview.

A Résumé

MARY LEE HALE

Home <u>Address</u>   Campus <u>Address</u>
11 Top St.   45 Race St.
Newark, OH 43055   Columbus, OH 43210
513/267-4819   614/422-6866

JOB OBJECTIVE

   To obtain a position in an advertising or marketing capacity, with an
   emphasis in either product development, sales, or promotional strategy.

EDUCATIONAL HIGHLIGHTS

   B.S. degree in Advertising, College of Communications, Ohio State
       University, Columbus, Ohio--May, 1986
   Equivalent to a minor in marketing
   Cumulative grade point average: 3.48; major field grade point average: 3.6

RELEVANT ADVERTISING AND MARKETING COURSES

   Introduction to Advertising   Advertising Media
   Creative Strategy and Tactics   Sales Writing
   Advertising in Contemporary Society   Marketing Research
   Advertising Management   Marketing Behavior
   Advertising Research   Operations Research

PRIOR WORK EXPERIENCE

   Sept. 1985-   McBride's Pharmacy, Columbus, Ohio
   present   Cashier

   May-August   Industrial Techtonics, Weymouth, Ohio
   1985   Market Development Coordinator
                      --effected sales through personal calls and correspondence
                      --created a company brochure
                      --developed new customer contacts through correspondence

   August 1984-   Campus Daily News/Digest, Columbus, Ohio
   March 1985   Advertising manager and sales representative
                      --conceptualized and executed advertising plans
                      --persisted in efforts to maximize revenues through
                          generation of new clients and revitalization of
                          stagnated accounts
                      --motivated sales representatives to become more efficient

   August 1982-   Rosalee Apparel, Inc., Columbus, Ohio
   April 1984   Sales Clerk
                      --introduced to the challenge of sales through the
                          commission system
                      --developed the ability to relate to and meet the needs of
                          a wide variety of people

EXTRACURRICULAR ACTIVITIES

   Dorm Vice-President   Little Sister--Zeta Beta Tau Fraternity
   Volunteer Project--Blood Drive   Intramural softball and volleyball

        REFERENCES   INTERESTS

     Available upon request   Skiing, tennis, needlepoint

GLOSSARY OF USAGE

Many of the entries here deal with pairs of words that writers often confuse because the words look alike or sound alike. Ascertain the distinctions between these confusing pairs and then invent your own memorizing devices to help you make the right choice in a particular case. In all cases of disputed usage, the most conservative position on that usage is presented so that you can decide whether you can afford to run the risk of alienating that segment of your readers who subscribe to the conservative position.

affect, **effect**. The noun form is almost always **effect** (*The effect of that usage was to alienate the purists*). The wrong choices are usually made when writers use the verb. The verb **effect** means "to bring about," "to accomplish" (*The prisoner effected his escape by picking a lock*). The verb **affect** means "to influence" (*The weather affected her moods*).

allusion, **illusion**. Think of **allusion** as meaning "indirect reference" (*He made an allusion to her parents*). Think of **illusion** as meaning "a deceptive impression" (*He continued to entertain this illusion about her ancestry*).

alot, **a lot**. This locution should always be written as two words (*A lot of the natives lost faith in the government*).

alright, allright, all right. **All right** is the only correct way to write this expression (*He told his mother that he was all right*).

altogether, all together. **Altogether** is the adverb form in the sense of "completely" (*She was not altogether happy with the present*). **All together** is the adjective form in the sense of "collectively" (*The students were all together in their loyalty to the team*).

among. See **between.**

amount of, number of. When you are speaking of masses or bulks, use **amount of** (*They bought a large amount of sugar*). When you are speaking of persons or things that can be counted one by one, use **number of** (*They bought a large number of cookies*). See **fewer, less.**

as, like. See **like.**

because of. See **due to.**

beside, besides. Both of these words are used as prepositions, but **beside** means "at the side of" (*They built a cabin beside a lake*), and **besides** means "in addition to" (*They bought a jacket besides a pair of boots*).

between. The conservative position is that **between** should be used only when two persons or things are involved (*They made a choice between the Democrat and the Republican*). Use **among** when three or more persons or things are involved (*Faced with a half dozen choices, he could not decide among them*).

can't help but. Conservatives regard this expression as an instance of a double negative (**can't** and **but**). They would rewrite the sentence *She can't help but love him* as *She can't help loving him.*

center around One frequently sees and hears this expression (*His interest centered around his work*). The expression seems to violate the basic metaphor from which it derives. How can something center **around** somethng else? Say instead *His interest centered on his work* or *His interest centered upon his work.*

continual, **continuous**. There is a real distinction between these two adjectives. Think of **continual** as referring to something that occurs repeatedly (i.e., with interruptions). For instance, a noise that occurred every three or four minutes would be a "continual noise"; a noise that persisted without interruption for an hour would be a "continuous noise." **Continual** is stop-and-go; **continuous** is an uninterrupted flow.

could of, **should of**, **would of**. In the spoken language, these forms sound very much like the correct written forms. In writing, use the correct forms **could have, should have, would have** or, in informal contexts, the contractions **could've, should've, would've.**

data. The word **data**, like the words **criteria** and **phenomena**, is a plural noun and therefore demands the plural form of the demonstrative adjective (*these data, those data*) and the plural form of the verb (*These data present convincing evidence of his guilt. The data were submitted by the committee*).

different from, **different than**. In British usage, **different than** is more likely to be used than **different from** when a clause follows the expression (*This treatment is different than we expected*). In conservative American usage, **different from** is preferred to **different than**, whether the expression is followed with a noun phrase (*The British usage is different from the American usage*) or with a noun clause (*This treatment is different from what we expected*).

disinterested, **uninterested**. Careful writers still make a distinction between these two words. For them, **disinterested** means "unbiased," "impartial," "objective" (*The mother could not make a disinterested judgment about her son*). **Uninterested**, for them, means "bored," "indifferent to" (*The students were obviously uninterested in the lecture*).

due to, **because of**. Many writers use **due to** and **because of** interchangeably. Some writers, however, observe the conservative distinction between these two expressions: **due to** is an adjectival construction, and **because of** is an adverbial construction. Accordingly, they would always follow any form of the verb **to be** (**is**, **were**, **has been**, etc.) with **due to** (*His absence last week was due to illness*); they would always follow transitive and intransitive verbs with the adverbial construction **because of** (*She missed the party because of illness. He failed because of illness*). Sometimes, they substitute **owing to** or **on account of** for **because of**.

effect. See **affect**.

fewer, **less**. Use **fewer** with countable items (*Louise has fewer hats than Emily does*). Use **less** when speaking of mass or bulk (*Elmer has less sand in his garden than Andrew does*). See **amount of**, **number of**.

hopefully. Many people object to the use of **hopefully** in the sense of "it is to be hoped," as in the sentence *Hopefully, we can finish our term papers by the deadline*. If you want to avoid offending those who object to this usage, you will rewrite a sentence like the one above to read *We hope that we can finish our term papers by the deadline*.

human, humans. Those who take a conservative view of language have not yet accepted **human** or **humans** as a noun. They would rewrite *The natives made no distinction between animals and humans* as *The natives made no distinction between animals and human beings*. In their view, **human** should be used only as an adjective.

imply, infer. There is a definite difference in meaning between these two verbs. **Imply** means "to hint at," "to suggest" (*She implied that she wouldn't come to his party*). **Infer** means "to deduce," "to draw a conclusion from" (*He inferred from the look on her face that she wouldn't come to his party*).

kind of, sort of. Do not use the article **a** or **an** with either of these phrases (*He suffered some kind of a heart attack. She got the sort of an ovation she deserved*). **Kind of** and **sort of** in the sense of "rather" or "somewhat" (*He was kind of annoyed with his teacher*) should be reserved for an informal or a colloquial context.

lend, loan. The conservative position is that **loan** should be used exclusively as a noun (*He took out a loan from the bank*) and that **lend** should be used exclusively as a verb (*The bank lends him the down payment*).

less. See **fewer**.

lie, lay. Lie (past tense **lay**, past participle **lain**) is an intransitive verb meaning "to rest," "to recline" (*The book lies on the table. The book lay there yesterday. It has lain there for three days*). **Lay** (past tense **laid**, past participle **laid**) is a transitive verb (i.e., must be followed by an object) meaning "to put down" (*She lays the book on the table. Yesterday she laid the book on the mantelpiece*).

like, as. Avoid the use of **like** as a subordinating conjunction (*At a party, he behaves like he does in church*). Use **like** exclusively as a preposition (*At a party, he behaves like a prude*). **As** is the appropriate subordinating conjunction with clauses (*At a party, he behaves as he does in church*).

literally. Originally, **literally** was used as an adverb meaning the opposite of **figuratively**. In recent years, some people have been using the word as an intensifier (*She literally blew her top*). Careful writers still use the word in its original sense of "actually" (*The mother literally washed out her son's mouth with soap*).

loose, **lose**. These common words look alike but do not sound alike, and they differ in meaning (**loose**, unfastened; **lose**, mislay). Here is a device to help you remember the difference in meaning. The two *o*'s in **loose** are like two marbles dumped out of a can (*The dog broke its leash and ran loose in the backyard*). The word **lose** has lost one of its *o*'s (*I always lose my wallet when I go to a carnival*). If these memorizing devices do not help you keep the two words straight, invent your own device.

past, **passed**. These words are more sound-alikes than look-alikes. The word with the *-ed* is the only one that can be used as a verb (*His car passed mine on the freeway*). The word **past** is versatile: it can be used as a noun (*I recalled my sordid past*), as an adjective (*I recalled the past events*), and as a preposition (*His car sped past mine like a bullet*), but it is never used as a verb.

principal, **principle**. These words sound alike, but they are spelled differently, and they have different meanings. Whether used as a noun or as an adjective, **principal** carries the meaning of "chief." The chief of a high school is the **principal**. The adjective that means "chief" is always *principal* (*The principal is the principal administrative officer of a* *high school*). The word **principle** is used only as a noun and means "rule," "law" (*A manufacturer shouldn't ignore the basic principles of physics*).

quote(s). In formal contexts, use **quotation(s)** instead of the colloquial contraction **quote(s).**

reason is because. This phrasing constitutes an example of faulty predication (see section **40**). Write *The reason is that . . .*

reason why. This phrasing is redundant. Instead of writing *The reason why I am unhappy is that I lost my wallet,* drop the redundant **why** and write *The reason I am unhappy is that I lost my wallet.*

respectfully, respectively. Choose the correct adverb for what you want to say. **Respectfully** means "with respect" (*She answered her mother respectfully*). **Respectively** means "the previously mentioned items in the order in which they are listed" (*Mary Sarton, Emily Doan, and Sarah Fowler were the first, second, and third presidents of the Guild, respectively*).

should of. See **could of.**

so, such. Avoid the use of **so** or **such** as an unqualified intensifier, as in sentences like "She was so happy," "It was such a cold day." If you must use an intensifier, use such adverbs as **very**, **exceedingly**, **unusually** (*She was very happy. It was an unusually cold day*). If you use **so** or **such** to modify an adjective, your readers have a right to expect you to complete the structure with a *that*-clause of result (*She was so happy that she clapped her hands for joy. It was so cold that we clapped our hands to keep warm*).

sort of. See **kind of**.

supposed to, used to. Because it is difficult to hear the -*d* when these phrases are spoken, writers sometimes write *He was suppose to come yesterday. He use to come at noon.* Always add the -*d* to these words.

their, there, they're. All three words are pronounced alike. The wrong one is chosen in a particular instance, not because the writer does not know better but because the writer has been careless or inattentive. There [their? they're?] is no need to review the different meanings of these very common words.

try and. In the spoken medium, one frequently hears utterances like *Try and stay within the white lines if you can.* Purists still insist that we write *Try to stay within the white lines if you can.* So if we want to be "proper," we should always write **try to** instead of **try and**.

used to. See **supposed to**.

whose, who's. Since the two words are pronounced alike, it is understandable that writers sometimes make the wrong choice. The word spelled with the apostrophe is the contraction of "who is" (*Who's the principal actor? Who's playing the lead role?*) **Whose** is (1) the interrogative pronoun (*Whose hat is this?*), (2) the possessive case of the relative pronoun **who** (*John is the man whose son died last week*), (3) an acceptable possessive form of the relative pronoun **which** (*Our flag, whose broad stripes and bright stars we watched through the perilous fight, was gallantly streaming over the ramparts*).

would of. See **could of**.

GLOSSARY OF GRAMMATICAL TERMS

Some of these terms are defined in the sections where they figure prominently. But since many of these terms also occur in sections where they are not defined, this glossary is provided for the convenience of the curious but puzzled reader.

active verb. See **passive verb**.

adjective clause. An adjective clause is a dependent clause that modifies a noun or a pronoun, much as a simple adjective does.

The relative pronouns **who**, **which**, and **that** often appear at the head of the adjective clause, serving as the connecting link between the modified noun or pronoun and the clause, which then follows.

The car, **which was old and battered**, served us well.

Those are the houses **that I love best**.

Sometimes the relative pronoun is unexpressed but understood:

The book **I was reading** held my attention. (Here **that** is understood: The book **that** I was reading.)

See **dependent clause, relative pronoun, restrictive adjective clause, nonrestrictive adjective clause, modifier**.

adverb clause. An adverb clause is a dependent clause that modifies a verb or verbal, much as a simple adverb does.

The subordinating conjunction (**when, because, so that,** etc.), which appears at the head of the clause, links the adverb clause to the word that it modifies.

When I was ready, I took the examination.

I took the examination **because I was ready**.

To take an examination **when you are not ready** is dangerous.

(Here the adverb clause modifies the infinitive **to take**.)

See **dependent clause, subordinating conjunction, verbal, modifier**.

antecedent. An antecedent is the noun that a pronoun refers to or "stands for."

In the previous sentence, for example, the antecedent of the relative pronoun **that** is **noun**. In the sentence "The mother told her son that his check had arrived," **mother** is the antecedent of the pronoun **her**, and **son** is the antecedent of the pronoun **his**.

See **relative pronoun**.

auxiliary verbs. Auxiliary verbs are those function words—"helping" words (hence, *auxiliary*)—that accompany other verb forms to indicate tense or mood or voice.

The following words in boldface are auxiliary verbs:

She **will** walk to work. She **is** walking to work. She **has** walked to work.

She **has been** walking to work. She **could** walk to work. She **must** walk to work.

She **was** driven to work.

See **voice**.

comma splice. A comma splice is the use of a comma, instead of a coordinating conjunction or a semicolon, between the two independent clauses of a compound sentence.

> He could not tolerate noise, noise made him nervous and irritable.
>
> *rewrite:* He could not tolerate noise, for noise made him nervous and irritable.

Since the comma is a separating device rather than a joining device, it must be accompanied in this sentence by a coordinating conjunction (here **for**), or it must be replaced with a semicolon

See **independent clause**, **compound sentence**, **coordinating conjunction**.

complement. A complement is the word or phrase, following a verb, that "completes" the predicate of a clause.

A complement may be (1) the object of a transitive verb (He hit **the ball**), (2) the noun or noun phrase following the verb **to be** (He is **an honors student**), or (3) the adjective following the verb **to be** or a linking verb (He is **happy**. The milk tastes **sour**).

See **transitive verb**, **linking verb**, **to be**, **predicate complement**, **noun phrase**.

complex sentence. A complex sentence is one that consists of one independent clause and one or more dependent clauses.

The following complex sentence has in addition to an independent clause two dependent clauses—the first one an adverb clause, the second an adjective clause.

> **When she got to the microphone**, she made a proposal **that won unanimous approval**.

As used by grammarians, the term has nothing to do with the length or complexity of the sentence.

See **independent clause, dependent clause**.

compound sentence. A compound sentence is one that consists of two or more independent clauses.

> He was twenty-one, but she was only eighteen.
>
> Young men are idealists; old men are realists.

See **independent clause, comma splice**.

conjunctive adverb. A conjunctive adverb is a word or phrase that links parts of sentences logically. Some of the common conjunctive adverbs are **however, therefore, nevertheless, moreover, instead, furthermore, consequently, meanwhile, in the meantime, for example, on the contrary, as a result, in addition**.

coordinate. Words, phrases, and clauses of the same grammatical kind or of equal rank are said to be "coordinate."

A pair or series of nouns, for instance, would be a coordinate unit. An infinitive phrase yoked with a participial phrase would not be a coordinate unit and should not be joined, because the phrases are not of the same grammatical kind. An independent clause would not be coordinate with a dependent or subordinate clause, because the two clauses are not of equal rank. An alternative term for **coordinate** is **parallel**.

See **parallelism**, **coordinating conjunction**.

coordinating conjunction. A coordinating conjunction is a word that joins words, phrases, or clauses of the same kind or rank. It joins nouns with nouns, verbs with verbs, prepositional phrases with prepositional phrases, independent clauses with independent clauses, adverb clauses with adverb clauses, and so on.

A coordinating conjunction cannot be used to join a noun with an adjective, a prepositional phrase with a gerund phrase, or an independent clause with a dependent clause.

The coordinating conjunctions are **and**, **but**, **or**, **for**, **nor**, **yet**, **so**.

See **coordinate**, **correlative conjunctions**, **subordinating conjunction**.

correlative conjunctions. Correlative conjunctions are coordinating conjunctions that operate in pairs to join coordinate structures in a sentence.

The common correlative conjunctions are **either . . . or**, **neither . . . nor**, **both . . . and**, **not only . . . but also**, and **whether . . . or**.

By this act, she renounced **both** her citizenship **and** her civil rights.

See **coordinate**, **coordinating conjunction**.

dangling verbal. A dangling verbal is a participle, gerund, or infinitive (or a phrase formed with one of these verbals) that is either unattached to a noun or pronoun or attached to the wrong noun or pronoun.

Raising his glass, a toast was proposed to the newlyweds by the bride's father.

rewrite: Raising his glass, the bride's father proposed a toast to the newlyweds.

In this sentence, the participial phrase **raising his glass** is attached to the wrong noun (**toast**) and therefore is said to be "dangling" (it was not the **toast** that was doing the **raising**). The participial phrase will be properly attached if the noun **father** is made the subject of the sentence.

See **verbal** and **verbal phrase**.

dependent clause. A dependent clause is a group of words that has a subject and a finite verb but that is made part of, or dependent on, a larger structure by a relative pronoun (**who**, **which**, **that**) or by a subordinating conjunction (**when**, **if**, **because**, **although**, etc.).

There are three kinds of dependent clause: the *adjective clause*, the *adverb clause*, and the *noun clause*.

A dependent clause cannot stand by itself; it must be joined to an independent clause to make it part of a complete sentence. A dependent clause written with an initial capital letter and with a period or question mark at the end of it is one of the structures that are called **sentence fragments**. An alternative term for dependent clause is **subordinate clause**.

See **independent clause**, **finite verb**, **adjective clause**, **adverb clause**, **noun clause**, **subordinating conjunction**.

faulty predication. A faulty predication occurs when the verb or verb phrase of a clause does not fit semantically or syntactically with the subject or noun phrase of the clause.

It results from the choice of incompatible words or structures.

> The shortage of funds **claimed** more money.
>
> The reason I couldn't go **was because I hadn't completed my homework**.
>
> *rewrite:* The reason I couldn't go was that I hadn't completed my homework.

The verb **claimed** in the first sentence is semantically incompatible with the noun phrase **the shortage of funds** that serves as the subject of the clause. In the second sentence, the adverbial **because** clause is syntactically incompatible as a predicate complement following the verb **was**.

See **predicate complement**, **predicate verb**, **noun phrase**, **verb phrase**, **semantics**, **syntax**.

finite verb. A finite verb is a verb that is fixed or limited, by its form, in person, number, and tense.

In the sentence "The boy runs to school," the verb **runs** is fixed by its form in person (cf. **I run, you run**), in number (cf. **they run**), and in tense (cf. **he ran**). The verbals (participle, gerund, infinitive) are considered **infinite verbs** because although they are fixed by their form in regard to tense (present or past), they are not limited in person or number. The minimal units of a clause, whether it is dependent or independent, are a subject (a noun phrase) and a finite verb:

> Bells ring. (but not: Bells ringing)

See **predicate verb**, **noun phrase**, **verbal**.

fused sentence. A fused sentence, which is a serious error, is the joining of two or more independent clauses without any punctuation or coordinating conjunction between them.

> She could not believe her eyes mangled bodies were strewn all over the highway.

Correct this fused sentence by putting a period after *eyes* and capitalizing *mangled*. A fused sentence is also called a **run-on sentence** or a **run-together sentence**.

See **independent clause**, **comma splice**.

gerund. A gerund, one of the verbals, is a word that is formed from a verb but that functions as a noun.

Because of its hybrid nature as part verb and part noun, a gerund may take an object, may be modified by an adverb, and may serve in the sentence in any function in which a noun can perform. Since, like the present participle, it is formed by adding **-ing** to the base verb, one can distinguish the gerund from the participle by noting whether it functions in the sentence as a noun rather than as an adjective. The following are examples of the gerund or gerund phrase performing various functions of the noun:

> As subject of the sentence: **Hiking** is his favorite exercise.
>
> As object of a verb: He favored **raising the funds by subscription**.
>
> As complement of the verb **to be**: His most difficult task was **reading all the fine print**.
>
> As object of preposition: After **reading the book**, he took the examination.

The latter sentence would be considered a dangling verbal if it were phrased as follows: After reading the book, the examination had to be taken.

See **verbal phrase**, **dangling verbal**.

independent clause. An independent clause is a group of words that has a subject and a finite verb and that is not made part of a larger structure by a relative pronoun or a subordinating conjunction.

The following group of words is an independent clause because it has a subject and a finite verb:

The **girls tossed** the ball.

The following group of words has the same subject and finite verb, but it is not an independent clause because it is made part of a larger structure by the subordinating conjunction **when**:

When the girls tossed the ball.

The **when** turns the clause into an adverb clause and thereby makes it part of a larger structure—a sentence consisting of a dependent clause (the adverb clause) and an independent clause (which must be supplied here to make a complete sentence).

See **dependent clause**, **finite verb**, **subordinating conjunction**, **relative pronoun**.

infinitive. An infinitive is a word that is formed from a verb but that functions in the sentence as a noun or as an adjective or as an adverb.

Capable of functioning in these ways, the infinitive is more versatile than the participle, which functions only as an adjective, or the gerund, which functions only as a noun. The infinitive is formed by putting **to** in front of the base form of the verb.

Here are some examples of the infinitive or infinitive phrase in its various functions:

(1) As noun (subject of sentence): **To err** is human; **to forgive** is divine.

(2) As adjective (modifying a noun—in this case, **place**): He wanted a place **to store his furniture**.
(3) As adverb (modifying a verb—in this case, **waved**): He waved a handkerchief **to gain her attention**.

The infinitive phrase in the following sentence would be considered a dangling verbal:

To prevent infection, the finger should be thoroughly washed.

rewrite: To prevent infection, you should wash the finger thoroughly.

See **verbal phrase**, **dangling verbal**.

intransitive verb. An intransitive verb is a verb that expresses action but that does not take an object.

Intransitive verbs cannot be turned into the passive voice. Most action verbs in English have both transitive and intransitive uses, like **I ran swiftly** (intransitive) and **I ran the streetcar** (transitive). But some verbs can be used only transitively, like the verb *to emit*, and some verbs can be used only intransitively, like the verb *to go*. If in doubt about whether a particular verb can be used both transitively and intransitively, consult a dictionary.

The following verbs are all used intransitively:

He **swam** effortlessly.
They **slept** for twelve hours.
She **quarreled** with her neighbors.

See **transitive verb**, **passive verb**, **voice**.

linking verb. Linking verbs are those verbs of the senses like **feel**, **look**, **smell**, **taste**, **sound**, and a limited number of other verbs like **seem**, **remain**, **become**, **appear**, that "link" the subject of the sentence with a complement.

Linking verbs are followed by an adjective or a noun or a noun phrase:

The sweater **felt** soft. (adjective as complement)

He **appeared** calm. (adjective as complement)

She **remains** the president of the union. (noun phrase as complement)

See **to be**, **complement**, **predicate complement**, **noun phrase**.

modifier. A modifier is a word, phrase, or clause that limits, specifies, qualifies, or describes another word.

In the phrase "the red barn," the adjectival modifier **red** helps to specify or describe the particular barn being talked about. In the phrase "ran swiftly," the adverbial modifier **swiftly** describes the manner in which the action designated in the verb **ran** was done. Phrases and clauses also modify nouns and verbs:

the girl **with the flowery hat** (prepositional phrase modifying **girl**)

the barn **that is painted red** (adjective clause modifying **barn**)

He ran **down the street**. (prepositional phrase modifying **ran**)

He ran **because he was frightened**. (adverb clause modifying **ran**)

Besides modifying verbs, adverbs also modify adjectives and other adverbs:

It was an **unusually** brilliant color. (modifying the adjective **brilliant**)

He ran **very** swiftly. (modifying the adverb **swiftly**)

See **adjective clause**, **adverb clause**.

nonrestrictive adjective clause. A nonrestrictive adjective clause is an adjective clause that supplies information about the noun or pronoun that it modifies but information that is not needed to identify or specify the particular noun or pronoun being talked about.

My father, **who is a college graduate**, **cannot** get a job.

In this sentence, the adjective clause **who is a college graduate** supplies information about the father, but that information is not needed to identify which father is being talked about. The particular father being talked about is sufficiently identified by the **my**.

A nonrestrictive adjective clause must be separated with a comma from the noun or pronoun that it modifies and is followed by another comma when the clause does not occur at the end of a sentence.

See **adjective clause**, **restrictive adjective clause**, **modifier**.

noun clause. A noun clause is a dependent clause that can serve almost every function that a noun or pronoun or noun phrase can serve: as the subject of the sentence, as an appositive to a noun, as the complement of a verb, as the object of a preposition, but not as an indirect object.

The subordinating conjunctions that most often introduce a noun clause are **that** and **whether**—although **that** is sometimes omitted when the noun clause serves as the object of a transitive verb.

That she would make the grade was evident to everyone. (subject of sentence)

He said **he would not come**. (object of verb; **that** is omitted here, but it is just as correct to say **that he would not come**)

The fact **that I had been sick** did not influence their decision. (in apposition to **fact**)

They asked me about **whether I had seen him recently**. (object of the preposition **about**)

See **dependent clause**, **noun phrase**, **complement**.

noun phrase. A noun phrase consists of a noun or a pronoun and all of its modifiers (if any).

In the following sentence all of the words in boldface would be considered part of the noun phrase, which is dominated by the noun **house**:

The big, **rambling**, **clapboard house on the hill** belongs to Mrs. Adams.

See **verb phrase**, **verbal phrase**.

parallelism. Parallelism is the grammatical principle that words, phrases, or clauses joined in a pair or in a series must be of the same kind.

Nouns must be coupled with nouns; prepositional phrases must be coupled with prepositional phrases; adjective clauses must be coupled with adjective clauses.

Parallelism breaks down, for instance, when a noun is yoked with an adjective or a prepositional phrase is yoked with a participial phrase. Parallelism has been preserved in the following sentence, because all the words in the series that serves as the predicate complement of the verb **was** are adjectives:

The engine was **compact**, **durable**, and **efficient**.

See **coordinate**, **coordinating conjunction**.

participle. A participle, one of the verbals, is a word that is formed from a verb but that functions as an adjective.

Because of its hybrid nature as part verb and part adjective, a participle may take an object, may be modified by an adverb or a prepositional phrase, and may modify a noun or a pronoun.

> Pulling his gun quickly from his holster, the sheriff fired a shot before the burglar could jump him.

In that sentence, the participle **pulling** takes an object (**gun**), is modified by the adverb **quickly** and by the prepositional phrase **from his holster**, and modifies the noun **sheriff**.

The **present participle** is formed by adding **-ing** to the base form of the verb: **pulling**, **jumping**, **being**.

The **past participle** is formed by adding **-ed** or **-en** to the base form of the verb or by a special spelling: **pulled**, **beaten**, **left**, **bought**.

The **perfect participle** is formed with **having** plus the past participle form: **having pulled**, **having beaten**, **having left**.

The **passive participle** is formed with **having** plus **been** plus the past participle form: **having been pulled**, **having been beaten**, **having been left**.

See **verbal phrase**, **dangling verbal**, **tense**.

passive verb. A passive verb is the form that a predicate verb takes when we want to indicate that the subject of the sentence is the receiver, not the doer, of the action.

The form that we use when we want to indicate that the subject is the doer of the action is called the **active verb**.

Only transitive verbs can be turned into the passive form. The passive verb is made by using some form of the verb **to be** (e.g., **am**, **is**, **are**, **was**, **were**, **has been**) and the past participle of the base verb.

The shepherds **tend** the sheep. (active verb)

The sheep **are tended** by the shepherds. (passive verb)

See **predicate verb**, **transitive verb**, **participle**, **to be**.

predicate complement. Some grammarians use the term **predicate complement** to refer to any noun, pronoun, or adjective that follows, or "completes," the verb, whether it be a transitive verb, a linking verb, or the verb **to be**. Other grammarians use the term **object** for the noun or pronoun that follows a transitive verb and reserve the term **predicate complement** for the noun, pronoun or adjective that follows a linking verb or the verb **to be**.

She is the **president**. (noun following the verb **to be**)

She became the **breadwinner**. (noun following the linking verb)

The pie tastes **good**. (adjective following the linking verb)

See **complement**, **transitive verb**, **linking verb**, **to be**.

predicate verb. A predicate verb is the finite-verb part of the verb phrase that constitutes the whole predicate of a dependent or independent clause.

In the following sentence, the word in boldface is the predicate verb of the independent clause:

The man **guided** the dogsled through the blinding snowstorm.

See **finite verb**, **verb phrase**.

relative pronoun. The relative pronouns **who**, **which**, **that** serve a grammatical function in an adjective clause (as subject of the clause, as object or predicate complement of the verb of the clause, as object of a preposition in the clause) and also as the connecting link between the adjective clause and the noun or pronoun that the clause modifies.

Who is the only one of these relative pronouns that is inflected: **who** (nominative case), **whose** (possessive case), **whom** (objective case).

See **dependent clause, adjective clause, antecedent**.

restrictive adjective clause. A restrictive adjective clause is an adjective clause that identifies or specifies the noun or pronoun that it modifies, that "restricts" the meaning to a particular person, place, thing, or idea.

> My sister who just turned twenty-one went to Ireland this summer.

In this sentence, the adjective clause **who just turned twenty-one** specifies which sister went to Ireland. If that adjective clause were enclosed with commas (that is, if it were a **nonrestrictive** clause), the sentence would mean that my only sister, who, incidentally, turned twenty-one recently, went to Ireland this summer.

A restrictive adjective clause should *not* be separated with a comma from the noun or pronoun that it modifies.

See **adjective clause, nonrestrictive adjective clause, modifier**.

run-on sentence. See **fused sentence**.

semantics. Semantics is the branch of linguistics that deals with the study of the meanings of words. As explained in the headnote to the Grammar section of this handbook (pp. 5–7), in order to make sense of any language, we must know the meanings of individual words (semantics) and the grammar of that language.

sentence fragment. See **independent clause, dependent clause, finite verb**.

stem form. The stem form of the verb is the form that combines with **to** to become the infinitive—**to walk, to go**. The stem form is also the same form that a verb has when it is used with the first-person pronouns in the present tense—**I walk, we go**.

See **tense**.

subordinating conjunction. A subordinating conjunction is a word that serves as the connecting link between an adverb clause or a noun clause and a word in some other structure.

The most common subordinating conjunctions that connect an adverb clause to the verb or verbal that the clause modifies are **when, whenever, because, since, although, though, while, as, after, before, unless, until, in order that, so that**.

The two subordinating conjunctions that serve as the link between the noun clause and another structure are **that** and **whether**. The conjunction **that** is often omitted when the noun clause functions as the object of a verb:

She said [that] the committee would not accept the proposal.

See **coordinating conjunction, adverb clause, noun clause**.

syntax. Syntax is the branch of grammar that deals with the study of how words are put together to form meaningful phrases or clauses in a particular language. Because modern English is not an inflected language like Latin, it depends mainly on word order to signal how groups of words are related to convey meaning. The phrase "the box big in" is not a meaningful unit in English; English syntax allows this arrangement of those words: "in the big box."

tense. Tense is that aspect of a verb which indicates the *time* of the action or state expressed in the verb. Here are the various tenses of the English verb, with an indication of how they are formed:

(1) **present tense**—formed with the stem form of the verb (**I run, you run**) or with **-s** added to the stem form in the third person singular (**she runs**) or with some form of the auxiliary verb **to be** and the present participle of the verb (**I am going, they are going**);

(2) **past tense**—formed by adding **-ed** to the stem form of the verb (**walk-ed, add-ed**) or in the case of irregular verbs, by changing the spelling (**go, went; sing, sang; speak, spoke; is, was**) or in forming the progressive tense of the verb, by using some form of the auxiliary verb *to be* and the present participle of the verb (**I was going, they were going**);

(3) **future tense**—formed with the auxiliary verb **shall** or **will** and the stem form of the verb (**you will go, we shall go**);

(4) **perfect tense**—formed with the auxiliary verb **has** or **have** and the past participle of the verb (**I have walked, he has walked, they have walked**);

(5) **past-perfect tense**—formed with the auxiliary verb **had** and the past participle of the verb (**you had walked, we had walked**);

(6) **future-perfect tense**—formed with the auxiliary verbs **shall have** or **will have** and the past participle of the verb (**I shall have sung, she will have sung, they will have sung**).

See **auxiliary verbs, participle, stem form**.

to be. **To be** is the infinitive form of the most frequently used verb in the English language, one that can be followed by a noun, a pronoun, an adjective, an adverb of place (e.g., **there, here, upstairs**), a preposition plus the object of the preposition (e.g., He is **like his father**), a verbal or verbal phrase, or a noun clause.

Here are the various forms of **to be**, as it changes in number, person, and tense: **am, is, are, was, were, shall be, will be, has been, have been, had been, shall have been, will have been**.

Some form of **to be** along with the present participle of the base verb is also used to form the progressive tense of the English verb: He **was going** to the doctor regularly. He **had been going** to the doctor regularly.

Some form of **to be** along with the past participle of the base verb is also used to form a passive verb: He **was struck** on the head. He **has been struck** on the head.

See **linking verb**, **predicate complement**, **passive verb**, **participle**, **tense**.

transitive verb. A transitive verb is a verb expressing action that terminates in, or is received by, an object.

The object of a transitive verb can be a noun or noun phrase, a pronoun, a verbal or verbal phrase, or a noun clause.

> They **destroyed** the village. (noun as object)
>
> They **shot** him. (pronoun as object)
>
> She **favors** giving me another chance. (gerund or verbal phrase as object)
>
> He **will try** to break the lock. (infinitive or verbal phrase as object)
>
> She **proposed** that everyone in the room be allowed to vote. (noun clause as object)

Only a transitive verb can be turned into a passive verb.
See **intransitive verb**, **passive verb**.

verb phrase. A verb phrase is a group of words consisting of a verb and all of its auxiliaries (if any), all of its complements (if any), and all of its modifiers (if any).

In the following sentence, all words in boldface would be considered part of the verb phrase (a structure dominated by the verb):

The army **has been severely restricted in its operations**.

See **noun phrase**, **verbal phrase**, **predicate verb**, **auxiliary verb**, **modifier**.

verbal. A verbal is the general name applied to participles, gerunds, and infinitives.

These words are called verbals because they are formed from verbs; because they are not finite verbs, they cannot by themselves serve as the predicate verb of an independent clause or a dependent clause.

See **participle**, **gerund**, **infinitive**, **finite verb**, **predicate verb**.

verbal phrase. A verbal phrase is a group of words consisting of a participle or a gerund or an infinitive and all of its complements (if any) and all of its modifiers (if any). In the following sentence, all words in boldface would be considered part of the verbal phrase, which is dominated by the participle **leaving**:

Leaving behind all of its heavy equipment, the army pressed forward quickly.

voice. Voice is that aspect of a verb which shows the relation of the subject to the action, i.e., whether the subject is the performer or the receiver of the action. The former is called the **active voice** (I loved her) because the subject *I* is the performer of the action of loving; the latter is called the **passive voice** (I was loved) because the subject *I* is the receiver of the action of loving.

See **passive verb**.

COMMONLY MISSPELLED WORDS

accept (cf. except)
accidentally
accommodate
acquire
acquaintance
address
all right
already (cf. all ready)
argument
arithmetic
athletics
attendance

beginning
believe
benign
business

cemetery
changeable
chief
choose (cf. chose)
conscious
correspondent

definite
dependent
design
devise (cf. device)
diminution
disappearance
dispel

effect (cf. affect)
embarrass
environment
exaggerate
existence

familiar
fascinate
flagrant
foreign
forth (cf. fourth)
fulfill *or* fulfil

government

harass

height
hindrance

incredible
independent
irresistible
its (cf. it's)

judgment

library
literature
lose (cf. loose)

maintenance (cf. maintain)
mathematics
minuscule
miracle
miscellaneous
mischief

necessary
neighbor
noticeable
nuisance

occasion
occurrence
occurred
offered
omitted

parallel
peculiar

possess
preceding (cf. proceeding)
prejudice
principal (cf. principle)
privilege

quite (cf. quiet)

receive
referring
relieve
remuneration
resemblance
reverence
ridiculous

seize
separate
similar
special
stationary (immobile)
stationery (paper)
succeed

than (cf. then)
their (cf. there)
threshold
too (cf. to)
tragedy
truly

usually

whose (cf. who's)
withhold

INDEX